Insanity

INSANITY

God and the Theory of Knowledge

JONAH HADDAD

WIPF & STOCK · Eugene, Oregon

INSANITY
God and the Theory of Knowledge

Copyright © 2013 Jonah Haddad. All rights reserved. Except for brief quotations in critical publications or reviews, no part of this book may be reproduced in any manner without prior written permission from the publisher. Write: Permissions. Wipf and Stock Publishers, 199 W. 8th Ave., Suite 3, Eugene, OR 97401.

All scripture quotations, unless otherwise indicated, are taken from the Holy Bible, New International Version®, NIV®. Copyright ©1973, 1978, 1984, 2011 by Biblica, Inc.™ Used by permission of Zondervan. All rights reserved worldwide. www.zondervan.com The "NIV" and "New International Version" are trademarks registered in the United States Patent and Trademark Office by Biblica, Inc.™

Wipf & Stock
An Imprint of Wipf and Stock Publishers
199 W. 8th Ave., Suite 3
Eugene, OR 97401

www.wipfandstock.com

ISBN 13: 978-1-62564-229-5

Manufactured in the U.S.A.

To Lenora,
Caedmon,
Margaret,
and
Pascal
—Four young philosophers who never cease asking why.

Contents

Acknowledgments ix

Part One: DESCENT INTO MADNESS

1 Introduction to Madness 3

2 Naked Skepticism 16

3 Beware of Skeptics Bearing Doubts 31

4 Cogito Ergo Sum 47

5 Philosopher of this Age 64

Part Two: ASCENT INTO KNOWLEDGE

6 Accidents of Reason 85

7 God Thinks, Therefore, I Am 100

8 Opening the Book of Nature 114

9 The Beginning of Knowledge 132

Bibliography 149
General Index 155
Scripture Index 159

Acknowledgments

INSANITY IS THE RESULT of many "insane" hours of reflection on the madness we live in when we fail to acknowledge God (the ultimate Knower) as both our source and goal of knowledge. This work serves as an introduction to epistemology, the theory of knowledge—one of the three traditional branches of philosophy (the other two being metaphysics and ethics). Though there are numerous epistemic resources available today, few introductions to the subject touch on religious knowledge as a tenable and worthwhile endeavor, and fewer still discuss the practical implications of knowing God rightly.

This is unfortunate. Epistemology is not just something to tamper with for fun. It shapes our world and carries tremendous theological and apologetic weight. No introduction to the theory of knowledge is complete unless it can integrate a coherent vision of the world as a whole. If our knowledge is not properly grounded in reality then, sadly, we are insane (as I will later argue). My ultimate goal in what follows is to demonstrate the need for an epistemology that is built upon, and substantiated by, biblical realities that culminate in Christ Jesus the Savior who is the ultimate Source of knowledge. After all, if our epistemology does not incorporate knowledge of the gospel, then it will implode, always pointing back to fallible human beings *i.e.*, madmen.

I can hardly hope to pass this theory of knowledge on to you, the reader, without expressing my gratitude to those who cultivated knowledge in me and who contributed in various ways to the quality and completion of this project. Douglas Groothuis, my professor of philosophy and apologetics at Denver Seminary, was instrumental in equipping me with the cognitive skills necessary to take on a philosophical project of this nature. His relentless defense of truth and unwavering commitment to knowledge

Acknowledgments

has helped bring me from the muddled thinker I was to the less muddled thinker I am today. Thank you for the knowledge you instilled in me.

My father Tony, a literary craftsman, gave me invaluable advice on the manuscript, as did my mother Gwen (Peacock). My brother Theodore, a gifted writer and student of literature, made many important comments on the voice and flow of the manuscript, eliminating some of the literary clutter. If any clutter remains it must be accredited to no one but me. I am thankful to belong to a family of writers who are always more than eager to discuss my writing (or any writing for that matter).

Sarah Geis, a skilled epistemologist, helped me clarify my thinking on several important points and helped save me from several incongruities I failed to notice. Donna Petersen did a tremendous job editing the manuscript and made many helpful comments. Thank you both. Likewise, my dear friend Ezra Alexander has spent more than a few hours discussing with me, nay, ranting and raving with me, about of the *insanity* we see in our world. Ezra, my time spent with you in conversation in the somber pubs of Stockholm, on the café terraces of Lyon, or anywhere else we happen to meet, is always refreshing, inspiring, and more valuable to me than you may know.

Finally, I wish to thank my wife Amy and our children. I am blessed beyond measure to have such a family. You have taught me invaluable lessons about God, the world, and myself. You have encouraged me faithfully. You have loved me much.

PART ONE

DESCENT INTO MADNESS

1

Introduction to Madness

HAVE YOU SEEN SUCH men—peculiar, raving, foam-mouthed, and straitjacketed—throwing themselves mercilessly at white padded walls while biting, spitting, and urinating on everything in sight? From the safety of your home, have you peered cautiously down upon the streets and seen these master prison escapists, capable of surviving jumps from third floor hospital rooms only to run naked through the streets chased by demons and invisible conspirators? They dwell in dark basements, afraid of light. Anything could trigger a seizure of their minds at any moment.

The sound of a B flat minor chord, the sight of a banana peel, or the scent of toothpaste could set off a rampage or leave them huddled helplessly in a corner. Drugged and wild-eyed they ramble in arcane speech, buzzing constantly about nothing and everything at once. These insane and maddened lunatics roam carelessly about the streets. They lurk in alleyways gnawing on bones and waiting to leap out of their hiding places and frighten your children. Sometimes wearing nothing but paper bags, they waltz into shops or restaurants, climb onto tables making strange announcements, dance a jig, and then retreat to the dumpsters in which they live. Others among the insane spend their days mumbling to themselves and solving enigmatic mathematical equations. They bark. They cuss. They drool. And they make themselves the brunt of jokes as they write poetry on the wall with their own filth.

In the stillness of the night they can be heard whispering secrets in the darkness of worlds beyond our imagination—worlds that only they

PART ONE: DESCENT INTO MADNESS

themselves have visited, where monsters lurk, and where men with hollow faces in white coats saw off limbs only to suture them back into place. Upon their return to earth they try to warn us, but to no avail. Does no one else hear the voices that speak so clearly in their heads? Does no one else see the demons that haunt them?

Have you seen such men? Or shall we speak of a different insanity—an insanity that leads some to jump from airplanes in full flight and to plummet headlong like lifeless sacks of grain until they have had their fill of exhilaration and open their parachutes. They jump also from bridges with elastic cords binding their feet and attached to the guardrails above. They leap so that just before they meet the ground and certain death they are snapped back up to safety. Wheels and velocity are the nourishment on which they thrive, and they live for the sensation that only near death can instill. The possibility of having to sit in one place for more than a moment is more than they can bear, and so again they throw themselves impetuously to the mercy of the laws of motion. These, too, are said to be driven by the insane ecstasy of some wildly preposterous feat or adrenaline-inducing thrill. In their recklessness they invent ways of scaring their loved ones half to death. We call them insane because they carry with them a certain propensity to carelessness and risk.

Have you seen such men? Indeed, one might claim that the mentally ill and the thrill-seeker are insane, but there are still other connotations to the word "insanity." Upon the completion of some great feat of strength, endurance, or flexibility, a performance may be described as "insane." In the same way, anything attention-grabbing, startling, upsetting, or remarkable is said to be insane. "That dance move was insane!" "That guitar solo was insane!" "That guy's hair is insane!" "She has an insanely beautiful body!" "My professor gives an insane amount of homework!" "Marry you! Are you insane?" Further, the accusation of madness is naturally heaped upon those with whom we do not agree or upon those whose recklessness invokes disdain or disbelief. Differences in behavior, dress, and political theory summon whispers of "Lunatic!" "Nutcase!" or "Deranged!" "He's not all there," we say. "He's off his rocker, out of his mind."

A WORD FOR ALL OCCASIONS

With so many uses, insanity begins to lose a bit of its luster. We no longer confine our uses of the term "insane" to those depicted in film and nursed

Introduction to Madness

by popular media and imagination. Instead, insanity becomes a word for all occasions. Anything and everything can be insane. Whether it is used as an allegation against the stability of one's mental state or as an exclamation of approval, the very idea of insanity carries with it suggestions of utter foolishness or of unsoundness of mind.

One who suffers from mental illness may rightly be declared insane, having succumbed to unreasonableness. Likewise, the thrill-seeker can rightly be declared insane by his evidently foolish exploits. A woman can possess insane beauty because of the stupefying effect she has on a man. A guitar solo can be insane because of the mind-boggling skill with which it is played or because it lacks any immediate explanation. Insanity is marked by a lack of sense, an inability to comprehend, and an indifference to reality. Foolishness, whether voluntary or not, is the core and essence of insanity. This raving, maddening, idiocy is pervasive if not pandemic in the world. Disturbance of the intellect is seen everywhere we turn and leads logically to a question.

If insanity points us to those who are careless, deranged, and foolish, then must it also point at each and every one of us? If insanity points to those whose beliefs do not fully correspond to reality and whose knowledge is dangerously incomplete, then must not madness point its finger at every individual of humanity? To some extent we all lie beneath the gloom of insanity, drugging ourselves into blissful ignorance by its poisonous fume. But there exists an insanity far more insidious and dismal than anything we are likely to imagine. More than a mental illness affecting the substantive matter that makes up the brain, this insanity is a condition that affects the immaterial realm of ideas. It is characterized by a lack of proper cognitive function and puts, therefore, a limitation on the knowledge one might gather, process, and communicate. Our shared insanity leads to the denial and misuse of evidence and the inability to comprehend truth. It affects the way in which beliefs are formed and leads to the denial of that which should be most clear. Right and wrong, good and evil, and truth and falsity are confused, then muddled, and finally, flat-out denied. In our madness, beliefs are formed that have little to do with what is real. Our insanity leads us to construct philosophies and ideologies that offer trivial answers to life's ultimate questions.

To call a man insane, therefore, is to claim that he clearly lacks both knowledge and the logic by which to make sense of that knowledge. The insane man sits in the shadow of an erupting volcano though he has been

PART ONE: DESCENT INTO MADNESS

warned by the experts to flee and though the sky above him begins to grow dark with ash. He reasons that he has never had a problem with volcanoes in all his sixty years in his humble cabin in the valley. *No crackpot scientist is going to tell him to leave his property. Of course not!* Nevertheless, this man shall be called insane. He has denied the evidence and chosen to believe the unbelievable to his very ruin. This blatant insanity is startling to those who consider themselves immune from such deliberate and unabashed stupidity.

The insane man is he whose moral categories are so confused that he elevates insects and wild beasts to greater worth than human beings. He comes to realize that the last step of the complex human mind is to realize its hopelessness and to kill itself in despair. He worships ideologies and denies truth, not because this denial makes sense, but because such denial is fashionable. He has lost touch with reality. His mind is corrupt and he is unable to process truth and form knowledge (Eph. 4:17–19).

The world is seething with untruth and confusion of mind. "Nothing is certain," it says. Yet it is certain that there is certainly no certainty. "Strong convictions are a menace and a danger," it shouts. Yet it believes this with unshakable and violent fervor. "Skepticism is a virtue to be upheld," it spews. Yet it fails to be skeptical of its own skepticism. It belches forth the poisonous claim that there are absolutely no absolutes and that truth is truthfully non-existent. Again and again these self-stultifying dictums are mindlessly chanted until the chanter believes the lie of his own making and is driven to further madness. It is these very men, drunken with insanity, who have become the judges of the sane, the writers of moral law, and the scrutinizers of true knowledge. What a wretched lot we all have become, dragging down what little sanity remains among us . . . down, down into the pit of stupidity.

Insanity, as we shall understand it, is seen, furthermore, in the mindless followers of propaganda or in the religious fanatic who pronounces doom on the world at the hand of a god of his own making. Insanity denies historical facts while spouting conspiracy and seeking ways to circumvent truth. It is seen in the ideologies, theories, and credos of scientists, philosophers, and practitioners of religious blathering who cannot see beyond their own hypocritical and inconsistent belief systems. Insanity, on a more subtle level, is practiced by anyone whose slew of inconsistent and incoherent beliefs about reality has developed out of a jumble of nonsensical and vapid aphorisms. Worse yet is the insanity that lingers in the mind simply

Introduction to Madness

as a result of the unwillingness to think, to reason, or to consider the consequences of an idea. Ignorance and intellectual laziness are both forms of insanity.

It is unfortunate, though not surprising, that all humans have fallen in varying degrees into a pit of insanity. Holding mindlessly to false beliefs, failed hypotheses, and unjustifiable ideas, each individual is left clinging for life to any root, branch, or outcropping that will prevent his plummeting descent into the dark abyss of folly. The gradual ascent toward knowledge is slow and arduous, and in the dark of this pit it remains difficult to ascertain just which way provides the best escape.

In their attempt to find enlightenment, some have wandered further into the depths of ignorance while others seem to be moving upward and hopefully out of the darkness. The difficulty faced by humanity is found in the fact that knowledge is essential to our survival, prosperity, advancement, and enjoyment of life. Ignorance is neither blissful nor welcome when one considers the vast wealth available in knowledge. For this reason insanity is not usually found at the top of any achievement list. The enlightenment of knowledge is much fairer than the muck of stupidity, and the need to know drives humanity much further than the empty appeal of ignorance.

When belief falls victim to indifference, and truth to lies, the sweet breeze of knowledge is replaced by a dispiriting blanket of hot air. Words wrought in knowledge cannot flow gracefully from the lips of the insane. These have been replaced with searing fumes. Harry Frankfurt defines such discourse as follows:

> When we characterize talk as hot air, we mean that what comes out of the speaker's mouth is only that. It is mere vapor. His speech is empty, without substance or content. His use of language, accordingly, does not contribute to the purpose it purports to serve. No more information is communicated than if the speaker had merely exhaled.[1]

As dismal as it may be, this is the condition of the insane. Indecipherable locutions drop like jumbled compost from their lips. Thoughts that lack truthfulness and justification—that are no longer believable—cannot be taken as knowledge. Like hot air, such thoughts are vaporous, if not excremental. Again Frankfurt says, "Just as hot air is speech that has been emptied of all informative content, so excrement is matter from which

---

1. Frankfurt, *On Bullshit*, 42–43.

PART ONE: DESCENT INTO MADNESS

everything nutritive has been removed."[2] Knowledge is not well cultivated in an environment such as this. And yet we sit in the waste pile while still clinging awkwardly to our desire to know.

THE WORK OF EPISTEMOLOGY

So persistent is the human need to know that we have even begun to ask ourselves how we know what we know. How can we be certain? What is our source of knowledge? Can we trust the beliefs we have held from our infancy? What constitutes true knowledge and what must be discarded? These questions surrounding knowledge and its acquisition are of great importance and their responses encompass what philosophers call *epistemology*, or the theory of knowledge.[3] The study of epistemology serves as humanity's best attempt to escape the insanity to which all of us are regrettably bound. This seemingly obscure discipline reveals humanity's desire to move from the dark pit of ignorance and intellectual inconsistency into the light of knowledge. The pit is deep, and you as a human being must emerge from its insanity.

From the time of Plato to the present age, knowledge has traditionally been defined as *justified true belief*. These three elements—Belief, Truth, and Justification—are known as the *tripartite* analysis and each must be held if one is to have knowledge.[4] For example, in order to know something, you must believe it. As I sit on a bench in the Musée des Beaux-Arts in Lyon, France, and look at the painting that hangs on the wall in front of me, I can claim knowledge that Henri Fantin-Latour, a nineteenth-century painter and lithographer, painted this beautiful piece entitled *La Lecture*. The piece depicts two young women, one of whom is reading from some kind of book. If I claim to know that this particular piece by this particular artist is located in the Musée des Beaux-Arts in Lyon but do not *believe* that such a painting exists, I have contradicted myself and do not possess knowledge. A proposition is not known unless it is believed.

2. Ibid., 43.

3. From the Greek words *episteme* or knowledge, and *logos* or science. Epistemology is, therefore, the science of knowing.

4. In his essay "Is Justified True Belief Knowledge?" Edmund L. Gettier argues that a person can possess a justified true belief and still not have knowledge. His famous counterexamples will not be addressed directly here, but I do hope to argue through the course of this book that we need not abandon the tripartite analysis based on abstractions and theories that hardly affect us in everyday life.

Introduction to Madness

However, the necessity of belief as a condition for knowledge is not sufficient. Belief must be aided by truth. In other words, in order for me to know that Fantin-Latour painted *La Lecture*, which hangs at the Musée des Beaux-Arts in Lyon, it must be true that this particular piece exists and has been mounted on a wall in Lyon's fine art gallery. In fact, every claim I make regarding the existence and whereabouts of the painting must correspond to reality. If no such painting exists, or if its actual location is at the Metropolitan Museum of Art in New York City, then the proposition is not *true* and I cannot have knowledge of it. Knowledge must be both believed and true.

But there is more. It must also be *justified*. I cannot have simply guessed the painting's creator, title, and whereabouts. My belief must be formed within a properly functioning cognitive state, in a reliable manner, and with good evidence. This it has, since I have viewed Fantin-Latour's painting in the Musée des Beaux-Arts in Lyon on many occasions (as I am viewing it now, while jotting these words on a piece of paper). Further confirmation of my knowledge has come from reading the informational plaque next to the painting and from discussing the painting's content with friends.

This standard tripartite analysis remains the best means by which to define knowledge, though some philosophers have sought to complete and solidify the definition of knowledge by adding other criteria. Based on certain criticisms of the tripartite analysis, and of *justification* especially, *warrant* has been used by some philosophers as a replacement for the traditional definition of knowledge. Alvin Plantinga notes that "a belief has warrant only if it is produced by cognitive faculties that are functioning properly, subject to no disorder or dysfunction."[5] These faculties must exist in an environment conducive to gaining knowledge, and they must exist under a design plan successfully aimed at truth.[6] In this case, any knowledge I have of Fantin-Latour's painting depends on the lucidity of my mind while viewing it, and on the presupposition that both my mind and my environment permit truth to exist and be discovered. In this view, our capacity to know anything presupposes a designer who is the source of knowledge and who creates minds capable of knowledge. If the designer is missing, our knowledge is left either to the despair of skepticism, or the endless and meaningless searching of autonomous human reason alone.

---

5. Plantinga, *Warranted Christian Belief*, 153.
6. Ibid., 153–61.

PART ONE: DESCENT INTO MADNESS

Both *warrant* and the tripartite analysis require that certain elements be put in order if anyone is to claim knowledge. Knowing requires clarity of thought, adequate reasons for belief, and the existence of truth.

Right knowledge is of great importance and should never be deposed by cerebral soot but sought after with vigilance. Having outlined intellectual rubbish many years ago, Bertrand Russell drew this conclusion: "Thinking that you know when in fact you don't is a fatal mistake, to which we are all prone."[7] With this in mind, I would like to repeat all the louder my audacious proposal that the human condition is one of insanity, precisely because our human nature has put a damper on our ability to know. When we rely on our own knowledge-gaining capacities we are easily deceived, lacking justification at times and failing to function properly. We hold false beliefs, we fail to search for truth, we convince ourselves of fallacy even against our better sense. We happily enjoy ignorance and we arrogantly claim to know truth when all we have are conjectures. Yes indeed, we are insane and should agree wholeheartedly with Blaise Pascal who observed many years ago that "men are so inevitably mad that not to be mad would be to give a mad twist to madness."[8]

I say this knowing that many will likely object. In rejection of this general claim to humanity's shared dilemma, it would be natural for many to obstinately protest with appeals to their intelligence quotient or academic credentials. But all credentials aside, there are realms that remain beyond our grasp. There are almost limitless historical facts that remain unknown, and as many scientific facts waiting to be discovered. Knowledge of future events remains ambiguous, as do answers to some of life's most important questions. The more we know, the more we realize how little we know. It is this lack of knowledge that contributes to our insanity. Our knowledge is limited and our cognitive functions can do little to relieve the problem, no matter how well they may operate. Even the systems of knowledge on which we rely are susceptible to doubt and repudiation. The first eighteen years of a child's life are spent in an educational system dedicated to the teaching of the basic laws of logic—two plus two is four, the green circle matches the other green circle, if Smith is correct that there is no God then Jones is incorrect that there is a God. But many children will go away to the university only to be instructed by their "wise" and "erudite" professors that all those rules they learned in school may be thrown out the window

7. Russell, "Outline of Intellectual Rubbish," 201.
8. Pascal, *Pensées*, 412/414; 120.

Introduction to Madness

and replaced with the "real knowledge" that there *is* no real knowledge, or knowable mathematical principles, or even green circles. "Nothing is knowable," they say. That is, all disciplines and systems of knowledge are ephemeral, illusory, and useless to the informed individual. In other words, children are being taught a form of insanity rather than being cured from it.

But this only makes sense. Why shouldn't the insane teach their insanity to the next generation? If insanity is all that is known or practiced, it is only logical that it is deposited on the hopeless children of each generation. Even the epistemologist, whose job it is to discover and defend knowledge, is often confounded by the bottomless pit of counterexamples just waiting to prove his theorems false. Insanity is the curse of both those who embrace it and those who defy it. How then shall we move out of the darkness of insanity and into the light of knowledge? How shall we human creatures—limited in reason, lacking in knowledge, and restricted in cognitive capacity—ever show ourselves cured from the phantoms that haunt us?

How shall we leave our straitjackets behind, wipe the foam from our mouths, and walk civilly through the door of our asylum and into a world of knowledge and clear thinking? How shall we begin to possess knowledge, to trust our knowledge, and to use this knowledge for our own betterment and the betterment of others?

The questions above are among the most fundamental questions a person can ask. The theory of knowledge must not be dismissed as unintelligible gobbledygook or time-wasting philosophizing. There are *not* more important things to do with one's time. If knowledge and its criteria cannot be established, then what is the use in asking the important questions in life: Is there life after death? Is there a God? What is my moral responsibility to my neighbor? How do I even know that I have a real neighbor? Can I trust the perceived reality in which I live? Am I nothing more than a brain in a vat, manipulated and controlled by a force that is beyond me? How do I avoid mindlessly believing whatever happens to present itself to me, be it an illusion, a dream, or a chimera?

A WORTHY DISCIPLINE

I would like to propose that the study of epistemology not be limited to some few philosophers, locked away at the ends of dark corridors in the back of university libraries. Nor should the questions posed within this discipline be dismissed as esoteric quantities far removed from the workings of life. What we must discover is the usefulness and beauty of knowledge. We must initiate ourselves to questions that far outweigh "what shall I eat this afternoon?" Or, "on what diversion machine or electronic device shall I waste my time today?" Food is, by all means, necessary. Entertainment is *not* inherently evil and destructive. But should we not seek a transformation and renewing of the mind (Rom. 12:1–2)? Knowledge is not to be taken lightly, nor is intellectual lethargy to have a place in anyone's life. Remember that we all live under the curse of insanity. Have we not accepted our responsibility, which is to seek the sane and reasonable way? Might we dare to view Christian theism as a tenable response to humanity's burning epistemic questions? We cannot rest forever in our fantasy of doubt, for there is something far greater that awaits those who search for certainty and who try to find a truly livable knowledge.

When Aristotle opened his great work, *Metaphysics*, by saying, "man by nature desires to know," he spoke of a truth that cannot be denied. This desire should burn powerfully in the hearts of Christians and non-Christians alike. To possess knowledge we must all seek the object of knowledge and source of knowledge. In doing this, our responsibility takes on many forms. We must understand our skepticism that we might know both the merits and limitations of it. We must consider the possibilities of knowing both our own minds and the external world. We must reflect on the criteria for knowledge and ask ourselves how sin and its effects have tarnished or even disabled the full capacities of the mind.

Finally, we must recognize the fullness of God's knowledge and savor the certainty that comes only from a source of knowledge outside us. Having done this, we may then grasp the hand extended before us and be hoisted from the abyss of cognitive aberration. We may safely put off the lunacy that impairs the world around us. True sanity must be our goal.

The main purpose of what follows will be, simply put, the explanation of a theory of knowledge informed by the Christian worldview. My purpose is to demonstrate the *sanity* of a "Christian" theory of knowledge by showing that the most reasonable theory of knowledge must be one informed by an understanding of God. That is, God as revealed both in his creation and in his Word, the Bible. Man-made systems of knowledge will only and always lead to insanity. True knowledge is something given to us, never something made by us. This is surely a bold claim that, for many, borders on insanity. However, it is a claim that I ask my readers, both Christian and not, to consider with utmost openness and honesty. We are liable to knowledge and obligated to truth by nature of who we are. So let us hasten to seek the truth, and in doing so, form a worldview that best allows for and values this truth. Truth is nonnegotiable. As William James puts it, "*We must know the truth; and we must avoid error*—these are our first and great commandments as would-be knowers."[9] Douglas Groothuis says this of truth:

> We seek it . . . and we fear it. Our better side wants to pursue truth wherever it leads; our darker side balks when the truth begins to lead us anywhere we do not want to go. Let the truth be damned if the truth would damn us![10]

How troublesome the truth; how bothersome and nagging our beliefs. The more knowledge we have, the more responsibility is thrust upon us. It is better, though, to seek after knowledge with a sincere heart than to be prodded and driven toward true beliefs like a clumsy and stubborn beast. This is the responsible and sane thing to do.

ACHIEVING SANITY

In order to establish the need for a God-centered theory of knowledge, we must examine the following ideas. My desire is to first demonstrate the limits of skepticism by examining the skeptical tradition and its contribution to the theory of knowledge. In doing this, I wish to demonstrate that skepticism is inadequate in producing satisfying knowledge without making the outrageous and arrogant claim that complete and final knowledge is possible in our transient lifetime. Yes, we live in uncertainty. Yes, we live more often than not without hope that our knowledge is true, or real, or free from doubt. But the skeptic, at his worst, has taken uncertainty even further, claiming that we cannot and never will possess any form of certain knowledge. Doubt is easier than certainty, and even certainty, when pushed by skepticism, buckles under the pressure that there is always one more objection waiting to bring it crashing down. The objections of skepticism must, therefore, be addressed.

Furthermore, I would like to show you the limits of purely autonomous human reasoning by demonstrating how reason alone fails to give us certain and definite answers about many fundamental questions. Pure

---

9. James, "Will to Believe," 1080.
10. Groothuis, *Truth Decay*, 9.

reason, if not guided by something outside the mind, will only *appear* to lead us to understanding and to the right way of living. It has been assumed that reason alone is the light that will guide us. But on whose reason should we rely? Pure reason may yield greater results and superior productivity than might skepticism, but such reason is debatably impossible, and is not easily defended in a world sans God. If autonomous human reason is the best way to achieve knowledge, then such reason must give us at least some level of certainty—certainty not limited to simple thoughts or sense perceptions ... but certainty that answers the difficult questions we ask about the meaning of life and our obligations as living, thinking beings.

In addition, as I open the second half of this book, I wish for you to see that *fideism*, or the conscious and complete rejection of reason in matters of faith, can do little more than further the creeping pestilence of an already decaying mind. To reject knowledge is to waste away in a hopeless mysticism by claiming that true understanding makes no real difference as long as faith has been activated in the mind. But here too, the beauty of faith is rendered unsatisfying when so rudely cleaved from its relationship to knowledge.

After addressing the scandal of skepticism, the recklessness of autonomous reason, and the flaws of fideism, we will examine the teaching of Christianity by showing how definite knowledge must come not from within us but from a divine *Knower*, namely, God. Without the certainty that comes from a divine mind, we will find knowledge to be largely impossible. Those who have succumbed to skepticism, those who are convinced of the limitlessness of human reason, and those who flat out reject knowledge are equally insane. Only when our declarations of knowledge are put in their proper relationship to God can we hope to possess knowledge that is justified, true, and constructive. By recognizing the proper source of knowledge man can take responsibility for his knowledge, using it to develop himself and others. The *knower* has a great responsibility that must not be taken lightly.

Commensurate to my main purpose is the desire to unveil certain common themes and essential concepts in the field of epistemology so that these too are accessible to all. Epistemology is not merely a branch of philosophical reasoning nor an abstract dimension of Christian theology, but a discipline that will ultimately help bring a great deal of clarity to our beliefs about reality. Any skeptic who claims to deny knowledge had better understand what it is he is denying and the implications of such. And any

Christian who claims to "know" God or to "know" anything of the world around him had better understand what it is he is claiming and why this claim is of such import.

What, then, can we know? How, then, can we know it? Have we any reasonable hope of throwing off the tyrant of insanity that leaves us raving madly in the dark? Ultimately, where does the epistemic journey begin? Ours shall start in the third century BC with a man named Pyrrho.

2

Naked Skepticism

Resolving to march across Asia on a campaign to rule the world, Alexander the Great led his forces to the threshold of India where he would subdue yet another kingdom. Among Alexander's host trudged a burgeoning philosopher who would later become known as the father of skepticism. His name was Pyrrho of Elis, c. 365–270 BC, and it was in India that Pyrrho encountered a group of strange Eastern wise men known as the "naked teachers." Exposing more than mere anatomy, these nude conjecturers revealed a philosophy of life that would come to oppose the ideas Pyrrho had inherited from the elites of Greek philosophy. Little is known now about the naked teachers, and less is known about what Pyrrho actually reaped from his encounters with them, but at the very least it is suggested that they influenced his theory of knowledge and led him to question the dogmatic certainty of the philosophers he had left behind in the West.[1] Upon his return home, therefore, he did what any philosopher worth his weight in ideas would do. He attracted some disciples and began to impart his brand of skepticism upon them.

Though Pyrrho may be considered one of the fathers of skepticism, it must not be assumed that no skeptical thought proceeded from the minds of men before Pyrrho began to utter his rhetoric to the waiting ears of would-be philosophers in the lyceums of the ancient world. Skepticism is, after all, a natural part of who we are as humans and already existed to some extent as an academic discipline propagated by the Sophists. It only seems

1. See White, "Pyrrho of Elis," 760.

Naked Skepticism

natural that we doubt and deny just as easily as we believe. Intellectual hesitations and suspicions seem almost sanctioned by the common inheritance of human nature, leading philosophers of every epoch to use various forms of skepticism and doubt to help verify their truth claims. Yet it was Pyrrho who truly developed skepticism as a veritable philosophy of life.

A COMMON INHERITANCE

The skepticism of Pyrrho was a deep-rooted inability to arrive at certainty. Even the *denial* of certainty was denied, leaving the skeptic devoid of knowledge and floating between the inexplicable nightmare of madness and the hope of ever possessing even the slightest understanding. For the Pyrrhonian skeptic, both ancient and modern, there is always one more question to pose and one more doubt to entertain.[2] Doubt after doubt, the skeptic must spiral down to the pinpoint tip of intellectual passivity. As Gisela Striker puts it, the Pyrrhonian is one who refrains from rigid or "dogmatic assumptions" about the world he perceives.[3] Likewise, he denies the possibility of justified true beliefs.[4] In denying this tripartite analysis, the skeptic unabashedly denies knowledge. The Pyrrhonian skeptic denies everything deniable, including denial itself. In doing so, he arrives at what he would call a state of *ataraxia*, or tranquility. In fact, Pyrrho and his followers looked to the complete "disavowal of knowledge" as a means by which to attain spiritual and intellectual peace.[5] For the Pyrrhonian, the worst intellectual sin a man can commit is to think he knows something. This sinner's only hope of salvation is in the gracious void of uncertainty.

Since Pyrrho did not produce any writings—at least none that survive today—we must rely on the later skeptics to both confirm and proliferate his doubt-abounding postulations. One such Pyrrhonian was a man named Sextus Empiricus (third century AD) who clarified the skeptical position by teaching that the goal of Pyrrhonian skepticism is to escape the intellectual

---

2. A distinction is often made between the "Pyrrhonist" or followers of the ancient school of skepticism, and the "Pyrrhonian" who may be a contemporary skeptic whose ideas are influenced by Pyrrho. Here, for simplicity's sake, I shall employ the word "Pyrrhonian" in reference to both.

3. Striker, "Historical Reflections," 14.

4. Ibid., 14.

5. Copleston, *Greece and Rome*, 413.

and moral troubles of the world.[6] Timon, another skeptic and disciple of Pyrrho, affirmed this by asserting the Pyrrhonian mantra that we can trust neither sense-perception nor reason.[7] And yet another skeptic allegedly added to this testimony the epistemologically haunting idea that "he was certain of nothing not even the fact that he was certain of nothing."[8] The naked teachers of the East had clearly left their impression on the Greek skeptical tradition by demonstrating the naked truth that there is no knowable naked truth.

Because of such radical doubts, the Pyrrhonian is left with no other intellectual end but to suspend judgment and enter into his paradisiacal state of ataraxia. This state of ataraxia is not something the skeptic willfully seeks. Nor would he claim that this blessed intellectual state is something for which he longs—as a Christian longs for the joys of heaven, or as a glutton longingly imagines his next feast. Rather, his tranquility is something into which he mindlessly falls. The Pyrrhonian, in effect, "does not conclude that he *ought* to suspend judgment, but finds himself simply unable to make up his mind."[9] He passively observes the world around him and floats carefree through life like an unmanned boat floating down a peaceful river. As Sextus declared, "those who hold the opinion that things are good or bad by nature are perpetually troubled."[10] *And who could possibly want that?*

Belief is always subject to doubts and speculations that ultimately tarnish the luster of certainty. But is it really possible to deny all knowledge and live in complete tranquility? Such thinking would certainly undermine the entire task of epistemology, whose goal is to "account for human knowledge of the world in general."[11] Epistemology, by definition, seeks inquiry into the nature of knowledge and justification of belief.[12] It is humanity's only hope for establishing reliable, warranted, justified, and true beliefs about reality. In contrast to this—and with utmost antagonistic fervor—the goal of the Pyrrhonian is to confound each attempt at knowledge by proving that no attempt can ever truly succeed.

---

6. Striker, "Historical Reflections," 15.
7. Copleston, *Greece and Rome*, 414.
8. Ibid., 414.
9. Striker, "Historical Reflections," 16.
10. Sextus Empiricus, *Outlines in Skepticism*, Book 1, Chapter 12, section 27.
11. Stroud, "Contemporary Pyrrhonism," 175.
12. Pojman, *What can we Know*, 1.

Naked Skepticism

Imagine sitting at a banquet with a spread of culinary delights heaped before you. The sight, scent, and flavors leave their unforgettable impressions on your mind. Of course, this is all very real. It is as real as real can be, for you have savored it with your own tongue and smelled it with your own nose. You have touched it. You know that what you see lies there enticing you as only a gourmet feast can do. But just as you are poised to relish another bite of an exquisitely seasoned culinary delight and wash it down with a swig of anything Bordeaux and grand cru, the Pyrrhonian demon appears on your shoulder reminding you that you cannot prove any of this. Your senses cannot be trusted, your reason is not infallible, your perceived reality is no reality at all. And what's worse, you begin to doubt the very doubts that have now implanted themselves in your already confused mind. What if you are eating nothing but gray paste and drinking flavorless pale yellow liquid? What if you are dreaming? What if your brain is being manipulated by an imagination machine? Your Epicurean experience is now dwindling away to nothing, and you will never again look at food with the same lusty appetite.

Perhaps you remember the doubts of Ebenezer Scrooge when confronted with the ghastly figure of his former friend and business partner Marley in Charles Dickens's *A Christmas Carol*. Scrooge could not and would not believe that the phantom before him was real. He reasoned that this specter was nothing more than a figment of his imagination brought on by a bout of indigestion. Why should he believe in ghosts? He had a near infinite number of counterarguments to justify his doubts about the existence of this creature. Why ever should he bring himself to believe in something so unpleasant when skepticism offered a much more intellectually safe approach?

When in doubt, keep doubting. This is the skeptic's creed. And then, when doubt has run its course, the doubter may be left with no other possibility but to suspend judgment and escape the mental turmoil before him. If Scrooge had allowed himself to continue in his doubts, instead of surrendering to the reality before him, he may have finished his evening in peace, neither knowing nor failing to know that he was engaged in a conversation with a repugnant apparition. With tranquility of mind he would have eaten his supper, wished the spirit a good night, and gone quietly to bed. What could be more satisfying?

Let the wine keep flowing; let the earth keep turning; let the gymnosophists bare their bodies, minds, and souls on the street corners; let yourself

PART ONE: DESCENT INTO MADNESS

engage the reality that seems to present itself to you and think nothing else of it. Nobody knows anything anyway. Go ahead, float through life in the ecstasy of self-inflicted ignorance and love every minute of it. What else could there possibly be? Perhaps the skeptic is on to something. Can we really have certain knowledge? Can we really think ourselves so grand as to have justified our beliefs?

Consider the book you now hold in your hand. The pages appear to you as smooth white sheets with black text laid over them in horizontal lines. But are you sure of the color? Are you certain of the texture? Are the words communicating meaning, or is it you alone who makes them say only what you want them to say? Is the book real? Are you dreaming? If you are dreaming, do you know that you are dreaming? Are there forces at work that control and manipulate your thoughts and make you perceive that which is not real? Is your sense of sight deceiving you? Is your experience of this very moment a mere illusion? Are *you* even real? If not, do you *know* that you are not real?

If the answers to these questions are as doubt-ridden as the questions themselves, then why act? Why go on eating and drinking, working and playing, reading, reflecting, and living your life? To this the skeptic may answer that ataraxia gives him the only reasonable basis to live. This may be, or perhaps he has simply lost his intellectual footing and tumbled headlong into madness. Perhaps he is left still clinging to the side of the deep chasm of insanity, unable and unwilling to move. But still he does not flinch, for he would likely respond by doubting both the existence of the chasm and the very possibility of movement in any direction.

Imagine that you are walking along a tranquil beach doubting incessantly and enjoying the ataraxia of the evening as the sun sets over the water. You stroll along admiring and puzzling over the seashells, crabs, and garbage that have been washed into your path, enjoying the fact that you do not know and do not care whether these things even exist. Suddenly, you see on the horizon a magnificent wave approaching the shore. At least you perceive what may or may not be a wave coming toward the shore. It grows larger and more ominous with every passing moment. Or perhaps it does not. You do not assert that the wave exists, that you see the wave approaching, or that the wave poses any real threat. You simply agree that these things appear. The wave grows larger, closer, and more terrifying. But you are a skeptic. How do you react? Should you react?

According to W.T. Jones, it must be understood that the ataraxia which these "arguments of the Skeptics were designed to achieve was not a suspension of action but of judgment."[13] Since action is allowed by the Pyrrhonian, the question still remains: How does one act when faced with a threatening situation? Can action be legitimately derived from suspension of judgment? Is not action a result of judgment? When your infant child is about to be torn apart by a wild beast are you provoked to action? Remember, you are a skeptic. You cannot know that the beast is real, that your child is in danger, or that you are even awake and not dreaming. If the Pyrrhonian runs for higher ground as the wave overtakes him, he has acted contrary to the doctrine of suspension of judgment. If he throws himself at the beast in an attempt to save his child's life, again he has acted contrary to his doctrine. Even Pyrrho, unable to divest himself from his own humanity, is said to have once climbed a tree to escape a belligerent dog.[14] But if the Pyrrhonian is to maintain his radical skepticism and stay his course of apparent ataraxia even in the face of such peril, then he has demonstrated nothing more than madness. He has shown himself insane (though such an insult would hardly move him since insanity, too, is subject to doubt).

Despite this shortcoming, there is a certain logic to the skeptic's case against knowledge. He claims that even the slightest doubt is reason enough to reject the thought of uncontested knowledge. Knowledge and doubt are, after all, incompatible. One cannot know something to be true while doubting his knowledge at the same time. This is like saying, "The ball is round but I don't know if it is round." If one harbors doubts of the ball's roundness, it would be absurd for him to claim certain knowledge that the ball is round. So again, the Pyrrhonian skeptic makes a logical case against knowledge by attempting to demonstrate the idea that all beliefs are susceptible to some form of doubt.

Even the less stringent academic skeptic, who under the influence of Socrates knew only his own lack of knowledge, has offered a weighty case against certainty. Academic skepticism was established in Plato's Academy (hence the title "Academic") in the third century BC by Arcesilaus, whose skeptical arguments were primarily marshaled against Stoic dogmatism. The Stoics held to a form of spiritual materialism. They believed that all things, including God, were made from physical substance. The Stoic God governed his universe through the laws of reason which, when properly

---

13. Jones, *History of Western Philosophy*, 351.
14. See Diogenes Laertius, *Lives of Eminent Philosophers*, Book IX.

applied, could gather definite knowledge about all things in the physical universe, including God himself. But for the skeptic, this intellectual audacity would not do. From the Academic school came the idea that any assertion of certainty was a monstrous utterance that must be quelled by doubt. In this sense, Arcesilaus went further than Socrates and joined the ranks of Pyrrhonism. Like Pyrrho and the naked teachers of India so many years before, the Academic tradition would set out to disrobe knowledge of her justification, exposing her susceptibility to doubt.

The arguments for skepticism were laid out by several philosophers of the Hellenistic age, but most notable are those of Agrippa (c. second century AD). Fredrick Copleston presents them as follows:

1. The variation of views concerning the same object.
2. The infinite process involved in proving anything (i.e. the proof rests on assumptions that require to be proved, and so on indefinitely).
3. The relativity involved in the fact that objects appear differently to people according to the temperament, etc., of the percipient and according to their relation with other objects.
4. The arbitrary character of dogmatic assumptions, assumed as starting-points, in order to escape the *regressus in infinitum*.
5. The vicious circle or the necessity of assuming in the proof of anything the very conclusion that has to be proved.[15]

These arguments settle most comfortably on the idea that there is no foundation, nothing fixed on which knowledge rests. Every so-called fact of knowledge is weakened by the countless opinions, ambiguities, and questions of justification. For every answer there is another question that tires and frustrates the mind.

THE PROGENY OF LUNATICS

We are the progeny of lunatics, and every generation of philosophers is burdened with Agrippa's maddening dilemmas—a philosophy of doubt, founded on an abyss. This long season of Pyrrhonian influences on the West have left it ripe to be harvested by another powerful force: Eastern pantheistic nondualism, the most common form of which appears in Buddhism. Though different in many ways, the Buddhist tradition mirrors that

15. Copleston, *Greece and Rome*, 443–44.

of Pyrrhonism in its doctrine of intellectual suspension and its quest for inner tranquility. All variants of Buddhism reflect the core doctrine of the Four Noble Truths that decree: To live is to suffer; suffering is brought on by craving and desire; suffering must be eliminated if one is to find peace; this state of peace comes by way of meditation, wisdom, mode of living, and so forth.[16]

The enlightenment of the Buddhist and the ataraxia of the Pyrrhonian are not far removed from each other. The goal is intellectual suspension and the prize is inner peace. And though the language may differ, as may the practice, the result is inevitably the same—escape from the insanity of an intellectually confused and troubled world. Buddhism is appealing for this very reason. Those who are religiously inclined may be drawn to a mystical escape from this convoluted world. A mind empty of knowledge provides that escape, both for the folk Buddhist and the academic doubter. What we don't know can't hurt us, and so the less that is known, the less harm will be done.

There is good reason to seek a tranquil life, free from burden, free from stress, and free from the pandemic cares of this toilsome life under the sun. Years before the birth of Pyrrho, the writer of Ecclesiastes muttered his gloomy outlook on knowledge.

> Then I applied myself to the understanding of wisdom, and also of madness and folly, but I learned that this, too, is a chasing after the wind. For with much wisdom comes much sorrow; the more knowledge, the more grief. (Eccl. 1:17–18)

The Ecclesiast (whose thoughts are reflected here) forsook the merits of knowledge, much like the Buddhist who would confound knowledge or the Pyrrhonian who would outright deny it. But unlike these two, the Ecclesiast later realized the despair that doubt would create. In the epilogue of Ecclesiastes, an observer looks back in reflection on the life of the Ecclesiast and notes at least one knowable fact that would have balanced his tormenting doubt, and that fact is this: knowledge of God.

The Pyrrhonian would likely find little problem pooh-poohing this fanciful idea as well. For him, all things, be they physical, observable, or thinkable, are subject to permeating and corrosive doubt. Skepticism of the knowledge of God is nothing new to philosophy as its roots may be traced back to the original naked philosophers—Adam and Eve. Many years ago,

---

16. Dhammacakkapparattana Sutta (Sermon on the Four Noble Truths), 82–83.

PART ONE: DESCENT INTO MADNESS

in a lush garden, there lived a man and a woman, or according to Christian theology, *the* man and *the* woman. Being the very first among humans, these two are said to have been created directly by God and endowed with the ability to think, to communicate, and to reason.[17] Not only did they possess knowledge of the world around them, but also knowledge of God, for God spoke with them, instructing them, and communing with them.

According to the biblical account, Adam and Eve were given their first try at skepticism when confronted with the enticing offer of complete moral knowledge. This temptation was presented by none other than the devil himself, who hissed several suggestions into the waiting ears of Eve while Adam stood by, dumbly watching, as his wife was seduced into sin. When first confronted by the devil's false information, Eve offered a challenge that hints at skepticism. The devil had spoken to her saying, "Did God really say, 'You must not eat from any tree in the garden'?" (Gen. 3:1). But Eve, now skeptical of the serpent's intentions, responded by correcting the devil's false information, though adding some false information of her own.[18] "God said not to eat it; God said not to touch it." Her response, for what it was worth, offered a good healthy dose of incredulity as she retorted skeptically to what she had heard. She was not about to believe this mysterious stranger on first contact. Her skepticism was directed against deception and lies.

But then her skepticism, like the fruit she was about to eat, turned suddenly quite sour as she moved her assault from the half-truths and deceit of the devil and toward the very source of knowledge—God himself. The doubts that should have protected her from Satan's ambush imploded into a self-destructing blow. And like a good Pyrrhonian, Adam stood by and said nothing, suspending judgment and going along with his wife's rebellion. He would later try to eschew responsibility by playing the innocent skeptic who merely followed the social norms of the society around him—the society being that of his wife and her serpentine collaborator.

What we learn from this event is that skepticism of false ideas lends itself favorably to knowledge. The skeptical tone of Eve's first response to the devil was skepticism of a half-truth, and it should have led to further skepticism of each and every bad idea presented to her that day. But instead, her

17. Their ability to think, communicate, and reason is evident in their dialogue with Satan in Genesis 3.

18. In Genesis 3:3, Eve correctly replies that the fruit of the tree of the knowledge of good and evil must not be eaten, but she falsely adds that the fruit must not even be touched.

skepticism took a wrong turn and she found herself doubting the reliability of her Creator and the knowledge that flowed generously from him. The skepticism awakened that day was a skepticism that would continue even now to the present age and plague the minds of all men.

Adam and Eve caused a monster of doubt to stir that would breathe its fume of radical skepticism over all humanity. The skepticism that led to rebellion against God was demonstrated in a malfunction of the mind. The first humans should have rejected anything that contradicted knowledge, for they had been given access to truth. They had walked in the cool of the morning in the presence of the very Source of knowledge. But instead of enjoying this privilege, they became skeptical of knowledge itself. It is no surprise, therefore, that those who regard the temptation account as an actual historical event also view misguided skepticism as a powerful and destructive force made to level any attempt at building knowledge. Once truth and knowledge were questioned by our first parents, there was no way for them to escape the cycle of doubt and there was no way to return to a state of knowing-only-truth.

From the first skeptical inclination sown by Eve and tended by her offspring, a dreadful tangled thistle of maddening doubts has choked the breath out of knowledge. For many ages, from Eve to Pyrrho, it thrived, until another two thousand years had passed and the Enlightenment brought new hope for knowledge. But this too was in vain, for another mad skeptic took it upon himself to perfect the Pyrrhonian craft. Like his first parents and their Pyrrhonian offspring, David Hume (1711–76) spun his web of skepticism over his predecessor's epistemic theories. The great thinkers of the Enlightenment—men like René Descartes, Gottfried Wilhelm Leibniz, John Locke, and Bishop George Berkeley—had attempted to solve the problems of epistemology and justify their knowledge through reason. But being the resilient skeptic he was, Hume would have none of it. He reckoned presumptuous any reasoning that attempted to explain anything beyond mathematical and logical truths. Philosophical certainty, metaphysical understanding, and knowledge of God by human reasoning were, for Hume, "the inevitable source of uncertainty and error."[19] He believed that since the mind deals only with the perceptions impressed upon it, it

---

19. Hume, *Enquiry Concerning Human Understanding*, 5. Metaphysical knowledge refers to knowledge of reality. However, this knowledge is not limited to scientific disciplines such as physics and cosmology. Metaphysics explores questions concerning non-physical entities and realities, such as God.

is incapable of distinguishing between those perceptions and the actual object of perception.

Hume's suspicions about human reason were confirmed in what he saw as a complete inability to reach certainty about the external world. If any link exists between reality and human thought, that link would always be inaccessible. And so Hume believed our perceptions must guide us despite their failure to give us a certain and coherent image of the world. You may open your front door and step out into the street, trusting that the dirt and stone from which it is made will not suddenly liquefy and engulf you. You may trust in the solidity of the street because the street has faithfully proved its solidity in the past. But you can never prove that the street will always remain solid or that there even *is* a street. Your perceptions may give you notions by which to live, but these notions are still subject to doubt. You will never know the true world that exists outside of your perceptions, for "the contrary of every matter of fact is still possible."[20]

Hume demonstrated the weakness of trusting in cause-and-effect relationships in nature by observing that even if the sun has risen every day since we can remember, there is no guarantee that it will do so tomorrow. If the impressions that lead us to believe in the fidelity of the sun are subject to doubt, how much more so are the metaphysical claims we make about the *self* or God? Hume asserts that such edifices are built from fanciful ideas laid on a foundation of doubt-prone impressions.

The world around us—if there is such a place—leaves its impressions on our minds. From these we construct the unjustified beliefs that lead to innumerable fictions that, in turn, lead to epistemic despair. But this was not the end of the matter.

Other thinkers, like Thomas Reid, responded to this Humean despair through the belief that skepticism must be exchanged for a common sense view of reality.[21] Hume's only hope of escape from the dismal Pyrrhonian conclusions of his philosophy had been found in his imagination and in the gaiety of dining, laughing, and conversing with his friends. Only the joys of life are powerful enough to divert the skeptic from the despair of his doubts. For when our friends bid us goodnight, when the effects of the wine wear away, and when we sit alone in the stillness of the late hours, we begin to contemplate once again the fundamental questions of knowledge. And the excesses of skepticism will lead us, as usual, to gloom and madness.

20. Ibid., 14.
21. See Reid, *Inquiry into the Human Mind*.

RESTRAINING SKEPTICISM

Pyrrhonism has its ugly side. To see it we must learn how to look more carefully through skepticism's diaphanous array—beyond the false promise of peace of mind and beyond the false hope of an escape from insanity. Skepticism only stokes the flames of lunacy. From its heart, doubts are pumped into every artery of knowledge. But is this enough to keep the hope of ataraxia alive? There is a contradiction that weakens skepticism's strength. One cannot simply float through life. One cannot simply abolish all desire. In suspending judgment, the Pyrrhonian must *know* that suspension of judgment is attainable. In throwing off the tyranny of desire, the Buddhist must in some way *desire* to pursue a freeing life. In doubting, the Humean must acknowledge the disappointment of facing a theory of knowledge that denies him pleasures that seem all too real. Even the first step toward skepticism requires knowing the reality of doubt and where it will lead. Without some knowledge of his own theory, the skeptic's philosophy of life would never even get off the ground. In order to fly he must first be cemented to the dogmas he tries so vehemently to avoid.

Knowledge, on some level, will be accumulated whether one likes it or not. Waiting in line at a bank or post office, we will see people around us. We will overhear their conversations, and notice their gesticulations. We might be sneezed on or bumped. We might be asked to move out of the way to let someone through the line. We might be tapped on the shoulder and asked for the time. We will react to these things in some way because we have no reason to doubt that the people are real and present and that our minds are working properly, allowing us to perceive the things that surround us. The skeptic will walk away from this experience with some new information or some new beliefs about reality. He will have reason to suppose that at least some of the recently transpired events occurred in a knowable reality. To deny this would be unreasonable.

But the unreasonableness of skepticism does not stop there. To claim that I doubt everything, including the fact that I doubt everything, is a claim to knowledge. That is, unless I claim to doubt the fact that I doubt everything, including the fact that I doubt everything. But again this is a claim to knowledge. No matter how deep a doubt goes, the doubter must always possess knowledge of his doubt. To avoid the infinite regress, the doubter must *know*, at least, his fundamental doubt. Already, Pyrrhonism has dissolved into its weaker academic cousin. The skeptic must know at least one thing: Skepticism is true. But if the skeptic knows something, namely, the truth of skepticism, then he has proven pure skepticism false by knowing something to be true.

Pure Pyrrhonian skepticism, as an abstract philosophical theory, leads also to problems of a more practical kind—problems that affect its livability. Claiming skepticism as a life philosophy may generate a kind of intellectual wonder in the academic world, but it hardly operates as a livable worldview. When a vicious dog bore its teeth, even the father of skepticism fled in fear. When the laborious chains of doubt were wrought in Hume's epistemic reflections, he, unable to bear their troubling weight, was forced to divert himself with a game of backgammon. Though the staunch skeptic may float tranquilly down the stream of life, doubting the rapids and rocks in his path, his doubt will not make them any less menacing. He must respond. He must react. He cannot hold the world in disdain or ignore the reality around him, whether he believes in it or not. Chasms, black ice, hornets' nests, and roaming gangs of robbers are not very helpful to the skeptic's position. Though the skeptic may try to doubt their existence, it is unlikely they will let him get away with it.

The Pyrrhonian lives his life according to the practices that surround him. He does not *know* how to act because he lacks the knowledge required to determine the superiority of one action over another. He eats and drinks only because that is what the world appears to be doing. He looks both ways before crossing the street only because careful street crossing is a common observance in his culture. But his indifference does not stop there. His moral categories are neutralized by his lack of moral knowledge. He will not murder, nor will he torture the innocent for pleasure, but only because these acts appear unacceptable in his society. His mindless compliance to societal norms disables any possibility of knowing objective moral principles.

The Pyrrhonian, like the Buddhist, must reject moral categories and ignore both positive and negative moral statements.[22] Instead, his moral conduct must be passive and determined by the social constructs that govern his life. To do otherwise would be to claim moral knowledge, thus treating skepticism with derision, which leads to irregularities in the skeptic's life and inconsistencies in his worldview. Any natural tug in any

---

22. One significant difference between these two is found in the Buddhist doctrine of *karma* which does not exist in Pyrrhonianism. The Pyrrhonian may participate passively in good moral conduct because of societal expectations, where the Buddhism may choose to abstain from doing good toward another for the sake of preventing bad karma for either party.

moral direction would need to be disregarded for consistency's sake, making moral ambivalence the mother tongue of Pyrrhonism. Unfortunately for the skeptic, such ambivalence does not offer a meaningful standard by which to conduct one's self and must ultimately lead to moral ignorance.

Even Hume's less aggressive skepticism leads to moral difficulties. For though Hume believed that morality develops within small family units, spreading into larger social entities, he could not ground such beliefs in knowledge of the reality or value of these units or entities. To be coherent, his moral theory must be consistent with the limits imposed by mere and feeble impressions. Yet morality must assume some form of knowledge and the certainty that comes from its justification. The closer one moves to moral certainty, the further he must move from skepticism about himself, about others, and about his responsibility to them. Without knowledge, the skeptic's attempts at morality are misguided at best and most likely prone to misanthropy (Eph. 4:17–19).

Skepticism asks us to test our beliefs, to get to the bottom of the theory of knowledge and see if there is any justification down there waiting to be pulled out. The bright side of skepticism is that it demands that claims of knowledge be backed up by conviction and certainty, and it requires the knower to defend his beliefs.

Beliefs must be tested, and it is the individual's responsibility to do so lest his natural gullibility lead him far from the truth. Unfortunately, humans are gullible, and we tend to like it that way. Testing beliefs requires a tremendous amount of time and effort. Yet, when the beliefs are not put to the test the results can be grave. Religious, political, economic, historical, and scientific beliefs when not subjected to a healthy dose of doubt can be adopted far too easily and can lead to horrendous consequences.

The travesty of blind acceptance must be tempered by questions that will lead toward truth and knowledge. But while Pyrrhonism delights in the questions, it does not like where the questions ultimately lead. It prefers to rest in intellectual suspension. Yet, Pyrrhonism itself has proved that Pyrrhonism is impossible. There must be an epistemic position more satisfying than that which the Pyrrhonian offers. There must be a way to justify our beliefs and gather knowledge. There must be a surer foundation than free floating Pyrrhonism.

While rejecting pure Pyrrhonism, many thinkers have been able to put skepticism to good use in constructing their theories of knowledge. The seed that Pyrrho planted all those years ago has indeed grown up into

PART ONE: DESCENT INTO MADNESS

the mighty Enlightenment project that sprouted during the Protestant Reformation and fully bloomed under the seventeenth-century Enlightenment philosophers. But as we shall see, the skepticism of the Enlightenment awakened the monster of pure reason, a dreadful beast that would fare no better in solving the fundamental problems of epistemology.

Have you seen such men—raving in the streets that knowledge is impossible and denying everything in sight including themselves? They lurk in universities and lecture halls, garrulously disclaiming knowledge and enticing others to join them on a religious quest for the land of ataraxia where all their cares will be lifted and where they will peacefully drift away to nothingness. They declare the end of knowledge and undo all the practical learning accumulated by their acolytes, sometimes through mocking and arrogant distain, sometimes out of despair and lamentation. "The history of ideas has led us nowhere but to skepticism," they claim, not realizing that skepticism does not lead to *nowhere* but, rather, to *somewhere*—somewhere quite dreadful. It has led to madness and proved itself unable to produce a satisfactory epistemology. The man of intellectual honesty, however, will accept the fact that the quest for knowledge may cause a few disruptions in his ataraxia, but he does not care; so be it. Skepticism does not provide meaning nor does it furnish an adequate means by which to understand the world. A more restrained form of skepticism must, therefore, be put to use in nudging the thinker toward *justification* rather than driving him to insanity.

3

Beware of Skeptics Bearing Doubts

As MEDIEVAL EUROPE SLUMBERED comfortably under the cozy quilt of dogmatic assumptions that had been carefully stitched together by the Catholic institution, a small and seemingly harmless trinket lay in its midst. It was nothing more than a mere token left over from ancient Greece—a few old scrolls that were being assiduously translated into the academic vernacular of the day: Latin. Marvelous things were now being read that had not been read for centuries, and more was being revealed by the day. Ancient works of insanity written in Greek and Latin were brought into the libraries of Europe and volumes were scribed that were once long lost. The works of Sextus Empiricus had been rediscovered, as had the writings of Cicero and Diogenes Laertius. The Greeks had left a gift that would keep on giving, namely the skeptical tradition. The gates were opened and in it rolled. The skepticism of the Greeks, though largely dormant for so long, had lain in wait until just the right moment, and then—when the world had grown fat and comfortable with its scholastic dogmatism—stirred, then sprang upon its now helpless victim. A new movement of philosophical skepticism was to emerge during the Reformation and reach its height in the Enlightenment, leaving even the contemporary mind shaken by its liberating and maddening effects.

Beware of skeptics bearing doubts—doubts that would upset the balance of a world dominated by the epistemic criteria established by the

PART ONE: DESCENT INTO MADNESS

papacy, upheld by the church, and practiced throughout Christendom. What Greek skepticism awoke in the late medieval mind was a simple question concerning the criteria of the day. Was religious truth to be accepted solely upon the basis of the word of men who claimed to receive direct and certain knowledge from God? Was religious knowledge as definite as had both peasant and monarch been led to believe? Though it would be a great stretch to assume that the doubts of the Reformers leveled against the Catholic Church were directly influenced by the rediscovery of Greek skepticism, it would not be a stretch to suppose that the rediscovery of Pyrrhonism during the Renaissance had created a climate where questions and doubts would no longer be restrained by the compliant sensibilities of the day.

A DRUNK GERMAN

The most famous supplicant of troublesome questions in the late Renaissance was a German monk named Martin Luther. Luther was a man desperate to understand his spiritual condition. He was honest enough to recognize that he was, by nature of his humanity, an unrighteous man who longed for the presence of a righteous God—a God of such perfect moral purity as to make impossible a relationship with something as soiled and ugly as man. He recognized his lunacy. His ability to know God was corrupted. His condition was that of insanity. This troubled Luther so much that he was driven to Scripture, so that in poring over it he was driven further still until he came crawling desperately to the threshold of an answer. He had come to the conclusion that all the imperfect works of righteousness he had stored up for himself, under the church's direction, were useless in the sight of a God who demands perfection. He could no more earn the love of God than dig through five miles of stone with a tin spoon. But beneath the spiritual questions that brought so much anguish to his soul were a series of epistemic questions that had to be answered if Luther was to move toward the hope he sought.

The questions being asked during the Reformation were not limited solely to those of biblical authority and salvation. Behind Luther's doubts about papal power were questions concerning knowledge. What source of religious knowledge was most trustworthy? On what epistemic authority could he know he was saved from sin? Could popish knowledge-claims be taken as justified? These questions forced themselves on Luther, rattling about in his head, besetting his agonizing spirit, and bringing him, stumbling, to the epistemic medicine cabinet. Here, groping for an antidote, he would find the healthy dose of skepticism that would prove to be his healing elixir—one tablespoon to be taken upon waking and washed down with a hearty pint of German lager. That was the way Luther liked it. But like any medication, too much can lead to undesirable side effects, as we have already seen with the Pyrrhonians. Yet Luther stuck to the prescription, and in doing so, reshaped the world of theology—and dare I say—epistemology, from the Reformation on.[1]

Luther did not begin, however, as a flat-out skeptic of the papacy. The doubts that stirred within his mind did not at first well up into rebellion. He carried on his daily monkish duties, both spiritual and carnal—praying, studying, performing the mass, going on pilgrimages, and drinking large quantities of beer, while doing his best to avoid the common medieval anxieties that came with the job. Witches, devils, pestilence, and rabid dogs were always a problem, but Luther had more serious problems to address. Questions of eternal consequence plagued him. From his work as a monk these questions began to circulate in his mind, and from the questions, doubts arose. It was not until, in an outburst against papal excesses, he nailed his Ninety-five Theses to the door of the Wittenberg Church.

The church, whether it admitted the fact or not, was in desperate need of Luther. But even in this protest, Luther had not yet jettisoned the papacy's criteria for religious knowledge. Richard H. Popkin suggests that "in his first protest against indulgences, papal authority, and other Catholic principals, Luther argued in terms of the accepted criterion of the church that religious propositions are judged by their agreement with the church tradition, councils, and Papal decrees."[2] Luther had been born and educated under the assumptions of the church, and though he was beginning to doubt its conclusions, he had not yet found the necessary skepticism to

---

1. I will admit here that it is always dangerous to make any dogmatic claim as to why one philosophy leads to another in the history of ideas. It is equally dangerous to pretend that Luther was in some way the reviver of Pyrrhonism when it is uncertain as to his actual contact with ancient Greek skepticism. My point is simply to suggest that in an age ripe for skeptical ideas, Luther capitalized on doubt as a means by which to confront what he perceived to be errors and excesses in the Catholic Church. In doing this, he sparked a reformation that affected not only the Church and world of theology, but all areas of science and the arts.

2. Popkin, *History of Scepticism*, 1–2.

doubt its methods. This skepticism would come later as pressure to recant was heaped upon him.

Until the Reformation, religious knowledge was determined by popes and councils. But these were composed of men—men who contradicted themselves and made unsound judgments, men prone to error and encumbered by the illusions of their own insanity. For Luther, religious knowledge could come from no other source than God himself. This led him to stand at the Diet of Worms and declare this:

> Unless I am convinced by the testimony of Scriptures or by clear reason, for I do not trust either in the pope or in councils alone, since it is well known that they often err and contradict themselves, I am bound to the Scriptures I have quoted and my conscience is captive to the Word of God.[3]

A new criterion for knowledge had been given. Knowledge of religious matters was to be defined in light of the conclusions drawn by the individual upon a careful reading of Scripture. The church's criteria were being replaced by those of Luther. He had proved himself more than a drunk German or wild boar in the pope's vineyard. He had unveiled a new world of skepticism where religious ideas could be tested by any individual willing to go to Scripture and examine it with care. God was now to be recognized not only as a source of religious knowledge but also as a guarantee of the validity of general knowledge about the world. A response to human nonsense had been proposed.

Surprisingly, the church's reply to Luther's apparent lunacy was to embrace a kind of skepticism of its own. Fighting skepticism with skepticism, the church's new skeptics made the claim that the Christian is better off to ignore the debates of theologians and simply accept the dogmas of the church.[4] Whereas Luther had eventually become skeptical of both papal decree and papal criteria, the church adopted a skeptical response to human knowledge and individual interpretations of Scripture. The church, guided by papal wisdom and tradition, knew best and should be trusted in all things. Luther's skepticism was thought to lead to a subjective faith built on individual conscience and compulsions. For the church, this was not a sure foundation. The religious knowledge imparted by the institution of

---

3. For a concise summary of the historical context surrounding Luther and the events that led him to his famous defense at the Diet of Worms, see Nichols, *The Reformation*, 25–38.

4. Ibid. 6.

the church was the only knowledge immune from the pestilential decay of individual interpretations of religious truth.

Luther, however skeptical of papal authority, was not stuck in his skepticism nor fixed on subjectivism. Rather, his interest, like that of reformers John Calvin, Ulrich Zwingli, and John Knox, was to establish certainty through the true knowledge that comes from that ancient good book, God's Word, the Bible. The act of knowing was of such importance to the Reformers that Calvin opened his *Institutes of the Christian Religion* by saying that "our wisdom, insofar as it ought to be deemed true and solid wisdom, consists almost entirely of two parts: the knowledge of God and of ourselves."[5] Knowledge was key, and the skepticism of the Reformers toward what they perceived as the faulty criteria of the popish throng served only to establish something sure: knowledge of God and of his creation by the truth of his revelation alone.

The Reformers wanted to demonstrate that the pope's criteria for religious knowledge were based on limited and incomplete knowledge, bad reasoning, impure motives, and malfunctioning cognitive abilities. Christian doctrine had been divorced from biblical authority only to take on the blind and unthinking acceptance of papal decree. What flowed from the decrees of the church's authorities were doctrines that, for the Reformers, reeked of works-righteousness and that were so opposed to Scripture and so offensive to the gospel that none other could be done than to cast them away into the apparent dung heap where they belonged (Phil. 3:7–8).

The theologians of the church were quick to bite back and squelch the skepticism of the Reformers with appeals to faith in the pope's good and divinely inspired resolutions. Erasmus of Rotterdam, in his response to Luther, had insisted on suspension of judgment concerning religious knowledge by appealing to "faith" devoid of reason. But for many of the Reformers an irrational faith was nothing short of the kind of insanity that only a madman would accept. Faith without reason was like icing without a cake.

The criteria for religious knowledge, which once seemed untouchable to the groping reach of doubt, were now subject to the ideas of Reformers, philosophers, and other intellectual rogues. Not long before, things had been quite different. For those in the Middle Ages who wanted knowledge, there had only been one place to get it: the Catholic institution. The established philosophical system was that of Aristotle, which was later adopted

---

5. Calvin, *Institutes*, (I–1), sec. 1.

and developed by Thomas Aquinas. Medieval scholarship assumed and absorbed the papacy's criteria for truth and by this truth a fortress of "knowledge" was built. This fortress seemed rather impressive to those who lived in its mighty shadow. Its ramparts loomed ominously above the ignorant peasants below until it was discovered that instead of stone and timbers, its great wall was made from scraps of paper pasted together. Lean on it just a little and it will begin to buckle. Apply a bit of pressure and it will break. The church had finally been found out. Its basis for knowledge had been built on the fallible and subjective intellectual whims of men instead of the unbending truth of Scripture. The Catholic institution was guilty of the same subjectivism of which Luther had been accused. Intellectual skepticism was again on the rise.

THE QUESTION OF CRITERIA

As the Reformation was taking root in sixteenth-century Europe, Michel de Montaigne, a French essayist, was busy reviving philosophical skepticism. Luther had turned the key to Pandora's Box and now all philosophical hell was about to break loose. Religious knowledge had once governed all other forms of knowledge. Theology had been the mother of all sciences. The truth declared by theology had once trickled down to influence all other disciplines. Now theological knowledge, or rather, justified true beliefs about Christian doctrine were subject to all kinds of doubt. Were these doctrines still beliefs? Yes. Were they true? Maybe. Were they justified? Never.

For Montaigne, Christian belief was whisked away to a realm of unreasonable faith untouched by reality. A dichotomy was forged that wedged, and then split, faith from reason. The reality left over—the world of matter and ideas—was subject to skepticism. New theories would replace old ones. New discoveries would abrogate established scientific "facts." New ideas would mock those that came before. The never-ending and vain search for something justified, true, and believable would propel itself forward with unrelenting zeal. Yet hopeless would be the quest for knowledge, like chasing the wind or catching a waterfall in a drinking glass. Better to let the cascade sweep you into the pool of Pyrrhonian doubt than to stand like a fool with your meager cup stretched out against the angry force of the water.

Montaigne was concerned with the problems surrounding criteria. In order to know, one must have criteria on which knowledge is built. But in order to have proper criteria one must know whether or not the criteria are sound. Roderick Chisholm puts it this way:

> To know whether things really are as they seem to be, we must have a *procedure* for distinguishing appearances that are true from appearances that are false. But to know whether our procedure is a good procedure, we have to know whether it really *succeeds* in distinguishing appearances that are true from appearances that are false.[6]

The quest for criteria creates a circle from which it is very difficult to escape. A beekeeper knows he is surrounded by a swarm of bees, but how does he decide how he knows? It would seem necessary for him to have some criteria in place before making the audacious claim that he is surrounded by bees. For example, he should know what bees look like and how they behave. He should decide how it is he can trust his senses. Yet, if he establishes his criteria for how to identify a swarm of bees, how will he be able to implement these criteria unless he already knows what bees are? For those who have given the question of criteria much thought, the circular reasoning forced by the problem of criteria proves itself less than sweet.

Montaigne's solution to this tiring wheel of questions was to retreat from the excesses of intellectualism. For him, man is vain and puny in what he knows, and he grasps nothing of the world that surrounds him.[7] What man perceives as knowledge is nothing more than a construct set upon him by the culture in which he lives.[8] Change the culture and you have changed the base of knowledge and in doing so, have subsequently relativized knowledge and solidified the grounds for skepticism. But what is this other than epistemic vanity? What Montaigne proposed in replacement of such vain pursuits was nothing new to the world of epistemology. What had worked for the Greeks of old would work for him, and so he suspended judgment.

Montaigne's response to the problem of the criterion makes some sense. Skepticism is a logical response to this problem sans solution. Which came first after all, the knowledge or the criteria for knowledge? If we say that the criteria came first, we are left to acknowledge that the criteria must satisfy the knowledge claim. But the knowledge that the criteria must satisfy the knowledge claim needs further satisfying criteria. The point is

6 Chisholm, "Problem of the Criterion," 9.
7. See Popkin, *History of Skepticism*, 45.
8. Ibid., 53.

this: Each successive criterion becomes a knowledge claim that must be backed up by further criteria. This creates an infinite regress of criteria. But the skeptic will not go down that road. He simply suspends judgment and avoids the question.

When faced with this dilemma, the only reasonable way to avoid skepticism is to concede that knowledge does not always need the backing of countless criteria. Some things can be known that need not be explained. If the skeptic is to truly doubt knowledge, then he must have a reasonable argument in order to do so. But to have a reasonable argument, the skeptic must know some things. And in knowing some things, his own skepticism is defeated. Furthermore, some things can be known regardless of how they are known. You need not always revert to a search for criteria in order to have confidence in your knowledge. Moreover, the skeptic has assumed that since it is logically possible for you to be mistaken in your knowledge, you must, therefore, be mistaken in your knowledge. But this will not do since the logical possibility of error does not necessitate the reality of error.[9]

In light of this critique, all of this talk of skepticism is essential to understanding the events of the history of epistemology. In launching into an examination of skepticism, it has been my goal to demonstrate the effects of this movement on knowledge. Thus far, however, skepticism has left us with an unsatisfactory solution to the problems in epistemology that contribute to our shared insanity. The project of the thinking human being must be to gather knowledge and use this knowledge to construct a coherent and livable worldview. He who lacks coherency in his worldview can never be intellectually productive, but is left only to his mad ranting. His words amount to little more than mephitic gas belched upon the world, like the vapors that rise from the mouth of an overzealous first-year philosophy student who raises his hand in class and boldly announces his nonexistence. You may be able to talk like a skeptic, but you can never live like one. And in this case, it may be best for the skeptic to simply stop talking.

An ancient Greek proverb implores its reader: *Know thyself*. But how are we to do this when knowledge has been forsaken at the hand of skepticism? He who is unable to ask the questions necessary to self-examination is unable to live, for he is unable to construct a life philosophy. He stands before the mirror but sees nothing of himself, only emptiness stretching on behind him. His raison d'être is lost in the fog of the nightmarish

---

9. For more on the critic of skepticism see Craig and Moreland, *Philosophical Foundations*, 98–103.

dreamscape that lies at the center of an impossible *ataraxia*. Here the horrors of a philosophical void await a mind that should never have failed to ask the most important question: *why?* The honest man, however, will seek to know. Unlike the skeptic who fears that which he might find lurking beneath the surface of his thoughts and who refuses to see his condition for what it is, the honest man will pursue knowledge with all its pains and pleasures. The honest man will seek to understand his condition of greatness and misery and will seek to know himself—a potentially frightening endeavor. The better he knows himself, the better he will know his fellow man and how to relate to him.

Know thyself then, and do so with the knowledge that the self is ever-present. The undeniably ever-present self is something from which we cannot flee. Though the mind is capable of much resistance to the perceptions that are presented to it, such resistance cannot be extended to the self. We are altogether incapable of resisting our consciousness of personal thought and self-awareness.

During his trial, Socrates is reported to have said that the unexamined life is not worth living.[10] Unfortunately, when skepticism is fully embraced, it leads to an unexamined life and on toward despair by failing to offer answers to any of life's ultimate questions. It ignores the questions and denies the answers, even when all of life hinges upon this exchange: What is reality? How do I know? What must I do with my knowledge of reality?

Moreover, when skepticism is taken as a worldview or philosophy of life, it leads also to insanity because it fails to give credence to the reality that surrounds it. It ignores the possibility of properly functioning minds, material reality, and interactions between human beings. It assumes the necessity of absolute certainty when absolute certainty has never been a condition for knowledge. It would rather suppose non-reality and impossibility than take as truth the things that appear so real. In other words, it fails to accept that which can be tasted, touched, seen, heard, felt, thought, dreamed, and understood, taking instead the ungrounded and fancifully mad idea that the only reality is no reality at all.

SKEPTICISM IN SMALL DOSES

The philosophy of skepticism might be easily equivocated to one who speaks while denying he has a voice, or to one who thinks while doubting

---

10. See Plato, *The Apology*.

that thought is possible. The skeptic contradicts that which is most evident. The closer he leans toward skepticism the more he eschews the real, and then, toppling as if in a drunken stupor, he falls away from reality and so loses something of his mind. He becomes an intellectual lunatic. All his formulas and arguments that look so good on paper offer him nothing of reality and prove themselves unlivable. This is the dark side of skepticism. Skeptical of his reason, the skeptic no longer has any reason to be skeptical. The skepticism of Pyrrho, Sextus, and Montaigne is intellectually frustrating. This form of skepticism does nothing for man but make him nothing. It leaves him supine in an intellectual wasteland, exposed to the ravages of a reality that exists whether he believes in it or not. I dare suggest that if the intellectual nourishment conveyed by pure skepticism could be converted into something truly edible, it would amount to little more than a stale breadcrumb.

On the other hand, skepticism in small doses can lead to some very fine intellectual breakthroughs. Self-examination requires a dialectic of questions, answers, doubts, and more questions. When skepticism was implemented by Luther and the Reformers, a movement of intellectual clarity was sparked that allowed tremendous progress in human thought that led toward the Enlightenment, or age of reason, as it is called. As we have seen, a small dose of medicine heals the body, where a large dose poisons and destroys. It is necessary to understand this if the swing toward the intellectual certainty of rationalism is to be appreciated.

The man credited with founding modern philosophy and combating skepticism in order to establish intellectual certainty was a Frenchman named René Descartes. If the Reformers set the fuse in place, and Montaigne lit it, then Descartes must be the explosion. Descartes' use of skepticism was intended to serve as a means by which to establish something more certain, and the late Renaissance skeptics gave him the fuel he needed to ignite this rational certainty.[11] Copleston affirms this, saying, "The revival of skepticism . . . is relevant to Descartes' attempt to set philosophy on a sure basis."[12] Descartes was a doubter of the established institutions, and like Luther, he was not content to rest in his doubt. Skepticism was, for him, a means to an end. It was a monster to be captured and chained. Sadly, monsters are all too plentiful in this world, and in the commotion of

---

11. Unlike Cartesian rationalism, which required absolute certainty, rationalism as a broader movement demanded only some kind of foundation or *a priori* knowledge.

12. Copleston, *Descartes to Leibniz*, 20.

subduing Scylla, Descartes awoke a hungry Charybdis. In the end neither was subdued. Now in the present age, rationalism and intellectual overconfidence—locked in a swirling fury with doubt and despair—have become the inheritance of a world post-Descartes.

Descartes was born in 1596 into a world of skepticism—a world recently lit ablaze by the Reformation. Eighty years earlier Luther's doubts were in their infant stage, and only ten years earlier Montaigne was still actively investigating all the possibilities of the recently resurrected Pyrrhonism. From a purely intellectual standpoint, this was an exciting time to be alive. As a young man Descartes began to doubt. He doubted the methods he had been taught in school. He doubted the ideas he had taken as knowledge. He even doubted the principles of philosophy he had acquired. He liked his newly found skepticism so much, in fact, that he began to doubt everything he had been led to believe. In doing so, he made it his mission to find truth by reason alone. Skepticism was to be put to immediate epistemic use by helping Descartes find just one fact of knowledge that could not be subject to its tyranny.

Like the stereotypical philosophers of our imagination, Descartes sat, hunched over a heap of rough papers, scratching his thoughts methodically with feather pen by the light of a candle in his drafty seventeenth-century lodging. This was indeed the philosopher-in-meditation, deep in thought while the divine aura of inspiration shown down upon him. But Descartes was also a man of the world whose restlessness took him from France to Germany and back to France, only to be led to Italy, Holland, and Sweden where, in the service of Queen Christina, he would die of a fever during the bitter northern European winter.[13]

Descartes' life work had been to attain epistemic truth by use of reason. Skepticism served him only as the means to this end. He began his famous *Meditations* by confessing the mental restlessness brought on by the incredulity that had long plagued him—restlessness that led him to reject everything constructed on the false premises he had acquired as a student. To be rid of all the opinions he had formerly accepted, Descartes was forced to take up skepticism and refute himself in order to find something more sure. He began by saying, "I will attack straightaway those principles that supported everything I once believed."[14] This would prove to be so great an undertaking that he purposely waited until he was sure he was intellectu-

---

13. See Copleston, *Descartes to Leibniz*, 64–65.
14. Descartes, *Meditations*, 60.

PART ONE: DESCENT INTO MADNESS

ally mature enough to accomplish exactly what he had set out to do. As he aged, the day finally came when he was ready to lay out his doubts one after the other, and so it began.

Anyone who sets out to doubt everything is quickly made privy to the fact that the mental energy required to treat every individual belief is not easy to come by. Who has time to sit and doubt every belief, unless you are one of those fellows mentioned in the first chapter who has been locked away for reasons of mental instability? It is much more productive to focus one's doubting on a handful of fundamental assumptions and be done with the whole mess of beliefs at once, than to suffer through lists of items that must be systematically doubted in order to arrive at the same conclusion. Incessant doubting can be a laborious and mind-numbing enterprise when performed with utmost sincerity and unrelenting consistency.

Consider the mental investment required just to doubt some simple inconsequential item like a lemon meringue pie. As you look at the pie and begin to doubt it, many thoughts must pass through your mind. Do I really see a lemon meringue pie on the table in front of me? Where did this pie come from? How do I know that the pie is real and not made from cleverly painted plaster? How do I know that I am not *dreaming* that I am sitting at a table looking at a lemon meringue pie? How do I know that lemon meringue pies are real and corporeal and not just imaginary desserts conjured up in the minds of hungry people? I was once deceived by a lime meringue pie masquerading as lemon. How do I know that I would not be likewise deceived today? I don't even like meringue. Whose idea was it in the first place to waste a perfectly good pie crust by filling it with this sticky goop? And why do I care? I have no way of knowing if my senses have rightly conveyed the impressions of lemon meringue to my now tired brain. Besides, what if I am being deceived by a clever scientist or a malevolent deity? What if I am being led to believe in lemon meringue when, if fact, I am sitting face-to-face with a mince pie, or worse, a pizza pie heaped with capers and anchovies?

These questions attack our knowledge of the pie in varying ways. Some pose a serious problem to the knower; others are largely irrelevant and question begging, and not at all related to the pie's actual identity and existence in reality. There is no end to the questions we might ask about the pie, and there is no end to the questions we might ask about every other thing that presents itself to us. But what is the point of asking all these questions when we could just as easily be rid of all the troublesome lemon meringue pies and everything else in one crafty maneuver?

This is the way Descartes saw it. Instead of picking apart the infinite particulars of the physical world, he decided that he would doubt the very possibility of knowing the physical world. Not content to stop there, he doubted the suppositions he held about the immaterial world—the realm of thoughts, ideas, moral principles, and God. He doubted that he could trust his senses for they had not proved themselves reliable in the past. He doubted that he could trust the existence of the objects around him for he doubted that he had any real access to them. He doubted that there was a Supreme Being who enabled him to trust his senses. In the absence of certainty, nothing was beyond the reach of Descartes' doubt. He doubted his own being and replaced himself with a brain in a vat controlled by a mad scientist. Even God was replaced by an evil demon that was bent on deceiving him to the fullest.

Doubt after doubt, Descartes tore down his world looking for one sure thing until he found it in the *cogito ergo sum*—the *je pense, donc je suis*—the *I think, therefore, I am*. This was it; he could not deny the fact that he doubted. If he doubts, then he thinks. If he thinks, then even if he errs in his thoughts he must at least *have* thoughts, as erroneous as they may be. Descartes realized it is impossible to deny thought while thinking. After all, "the proposition, I think, is one whose very denial proves it true."[15] As Gordon Clark suggests in his summary of Descartes logic, "I do not have to walk in order to deny that I am walking, but I cannot deny or doubt that I think without thinking."[16] The existence of thought is the essential point of departure. From this, Descartes reasoned that he, a thinker, could not have thoughts unless he existed. Doubt had proved to be his certainty. From this simple concept Descartes reconstructed knowledge from the ground up and rebuilt a rational philosophy that he believed was now immune to doubt's corrosive effects.[17]

Like Luther, Descartes wanted something sure, but unlike the Reformer, he looked for it not in God but in man. He himself would have to be the source of knowledge. From the *cogito ergo sum* he would construct

15. Clark, *Thales to Dewey*, 246.

16. Ibid., 246.

17. It is important to note that in his third and fifth meditations, Descartes employed an argument from mind for the existence of God. Though God's existence served as a foundation for his rational certainty, it was not his ultimate source for knowledge and remained secondary to the *cogito*.

for himself a ladder to the heavenly places of truth, and in doing so, leave the world of the cognitively impaired masses far below. From his perch he hoped that he would wave goodbye to uncertainty and breathe in the untainted knowledge he had sought.

GOOD AND BAD SKEPTICISM

Descartes served as a bridge between doubt and certainty. Knowledge was his ultimate goal and skepticism functioned only as a means to this end. Having now seen where Descartes' skepticism aided him in this, I hope it is clear that skepticism has its place in the world. Whether one agrees with Descartes' method or with his conclusions is irrelevant to the fact that he took a giant step in the field of epistemology. His philosophy shows us that doubt has its benefits as it can help us revise our truth claims, build knowledge, and test ideas. Likewise, doubt sharpens us, ensuring that we do not take for granted the knowledge we have. It allows us to confess that there are some things that are hard to believe and others that are downright unbelievable, and that we need not fear the consequences of a little incredulity. Skepticism, in moderation, need not be a source of discomfort for the epistemologist, nor a source of fear for the Christian seeking truth.

To uncritically embrace the wisdom of a fallen world is folly indeed. The insanity of its ethics must be doubted, and the madness of its philosophy of life cannot be trusted. To subject all ideas to clear and critical thought will almost always do you good, as long as you are willing to be as charitable and objective as your biased nature will allow. Skepticism, when carefully controlled, can lend itself to the construction of knowledge. This first form of skepticism should be employed in the quest for knowledge, as it has been employed in the past to the advantage of mankind.

However, there is a second form of skepticism, a pseudo-skepticism, which has found its way into the human intellectual tradition. It has become à la mode to flaunt skepticism as one might flaunt the latest trends in fashion. Skepticism is touted like a title or an advanced degree tacked to one's name. This grand and distinguished designation has become synonymous with such concepts as free-thinking, unconventional, intellectual, and informed-in-all-things-modern. Men who wear this new style are skeptical of institutions, religions, God, and moral absolutes. They are above such things; they are the *new* agnostics—the skeptics who need not be troubled with religious nonsense. Privileged with the uncommon knowledge that they must subject all things to distrust in order to put the "knower" in his place, they have embraced a fear of knowledge and have failed to doubt their own criteria for skepticism. They are skeptics, after all, and they will doubt every belief while failing to question whether they should doubt their *own* doubt and whether or not their *own* belief leads to anything more meaningful. These types of skeptics are not intellectually consistent. They are, rather, intellectually antagonistic and are not true skeptics. It is impossible that such men have ever thought through their position. They are more likely to have been fed their philosophical outlook by the media, by agenda-seeking professors, or by the clichés of the day. They eschew careful reflection. Mindless mobs are made up of such freethinking individuals (as they like to call themselves) who cannot grasp the implications of their inconsistency. Unlike the Pyrrhonian, these men are not to be taken seriously.[18]

The Pyrrhonian does, however, pose a real threat to knowledge. This third form of skepticism poses an unmistakable danger if we are not careful with our doubts. Unchecked, our trajectory leads from *skepticism* to *skeptic* and from *skeptic* to *madman*. A world filled with pure skeptics would be like a calm sea filled with little one-man boats. Their captains, like men in a trance, would slowly drift about bumping into one another without the slightest concern for anything. No cares, no worries, no meaning, no value, they would stay their course or lack thereof until they die and roll, with hardly a splash, into the water so to continue as before, staring vacantly skyward and bumping about indolently like corks floating in a wash basin. The proliferation of skepticism increases the denial that objective reality can be known.[19] And if reality is unknowable, then we cannot properly live in it.

The world in which the skeptic lives is unknowable and hence, unreal. His "real" world is one of doubt and suspicion where nothing is certain and where confidence in truth has been lost. It is a vague ghostly place of deception, uncertainty, and confusion. For him, any sort of truth, objective reality, or certain knowledge is removed to the realm of fantasy. Only in this dreamworld of the imagination can true and justified beliefs reside. The skeptic has inverted reality and fantasy so that truth is made to be a figment of the imagination. As one would suspect of the insane, he would

---

18. For more on the various forms of skepticism and their uses, see McGrew, *Foundations of Knowledge*, 3–8.

19. See Frankfurt, *On Bullshit*, 64–65. Here Frankfurt argues that excremental thinking leads to skepticism which leads in turn to "loss of confidence" in objective truth.

rather call the waking world a lie than wake up from his foggy dream of doubt. He would rather go on living without belief than believe something that *might* not be true. He would come to the end of his life and be able to say, "I was never right about anything, but at least I was never wrong either." He would stand in a whirling snowstorm and be frozen to death, rather than risk following a path that *might* not safely lead him home.[20] But what good would the skeptic gain in this? His doubts would have him frozen to death. I caution you then in your doubts. Doubt a little if you will. A few hearty suspicions may do much more good than harm, but be warned of skepticism's folly lest you be driven to madness.

The extent to which doubt serves humanity is itself subject to doubt, but never fear—you will not be miraculously transformed into a Pyrrhonian skeptic just because you doubt from time to time or approach new ideas with a critical mind. Man does become a skeptic, however, when he finds no solace in knowledge and drifts toward the Pyrrhonian ideal. Skepticism chokes out knowledge when, instead of pushing the doubter to firmer ground, it makes his belief smaller. Any belief subjected to doubt will either answer that doubt or wither under the weight of skepticism. Pure skepticism likes to challenge every knowledge claim until there is nothing left to challenge except the challenge itself. Ruined by the gambit of unremitting doubt, knowledge lies dead. And who is left to eulogize this lost love? Not skepticism, for it cares for nothing and would self-destruct by the poison of its own making. This too is insanity.

---

20. See James, "Will to Believe," 1080. James uses this analogy in the context of religious knowledge and faith, but I find it appropriate for this discussion of skepticism. Holding complete certainty in knowledge may be debatable, but there are times to follow the direction of the most reasonable path instead of standing lifeless in a judgment suspending stupor.

4

Cogito Ergo Sum

EUROPE WAS A MUCH different place back then, when half-starved wolves left the shadows of the forests, creeping guilefully against the lackluster grey stone, and slinking though village streets in mid-winter looking for scraps of food or young children to eat. And children, shivering in straw-stuffed beds, feared the unknown black of a dark haunted world. Elves and goblins, driven from the towns, still occupied the remotest parts of the wilderness. The faint chiming of their songs was now and then heard in the breeze, reminding travelers of their elusive presence.

Witches with grotesquely long noses, robed in black, were sometimes spotted dancing on distant ridges in the moonlight before taking flight or vanishing in clouds of murky vapor. Charlatans and illusionists traveled the dangerously pothole-filled roads following the scent of smoke and filth that would lead them to the next human settlement, where they could sell amulets that would protect their wearers from plague, hiccups, and flatulence. Toothless men sat in dark taverns, avoiding their wives, drinking gritty brown ale, and exaggerating beyond measure. The heads of condemned criminals hung from bridges and stared unflinching into eternity. The earth had only just been made spherical, but this had little bearing on the life of the haymaker as he sat resting in his field nibbling a piece of stale bread and watching the sun sink behind a church steeple in the distance.

Reason, long asleep, was about to awaken, to loosen her robe, slip from her diaphanous veil, and open her curtain to the waiting eyes of humanity. Enlightenment was in the air and the intellectual certainty it promised

PART ONE: DESCENT INTO MADNESS

would put an end to the superstitions and ignorance of the past. Man would now be free—free from the stupidity that had been worn shamefully by every former generation. His knowledge would be complete. Yes, a thaw was taking place. Men were coming back from the dead. Humanity had finally done it. We had made ourselves into gods-all-knowing, clothed majestically in reason.[1]

THE WORLD OF REASON

Have you seen such men? Descartes had done more than alleviate the discomforts of skepticism in the seventeenth century. He had done more than take a step in the advancement of philosophy. In fact, his thoughts would become much more than an intellectual trend, to be discarded carelessly by the next generation of thinkers. His work was far from trivial, and through his efforts he produced what would develop into generations of philosophers whose confident, and dare I say, arrogant certainty would prove little more valuable than the doubts of the skeptics. The skeptic is made insane, after all, by his denial of knowledge, and the rationalist by his unthinking confidence in himself. Yet, both are madmen. And this new madman, the offspring of the Enlightenment, poised and adorned in reason, may now declare himself wiser than every generation before him. Having cast God away in favor of science and reason, he will never succumb to religion and its blunders. For him, the swindling black-souled clergy and bickering theologians who slink through the murky halls of gothic ruins have no place in this new world where men of reason now reign.[2]

---

    1. It has been long assumed that medieval people were ignorant superstitious fools who still lived in the Stone Age: an age into which they had been thrust after the fall of the Roman Empire. It is thought that these poor wretches were unable to fully recover until the Renaissance and Enlightenment had run their courses, transitioning man into modernity. This assumption, however, is far from the truth. Did superstitions exist? Yes, as they do today. Were people well informed and capable of great achievements? No less than they are in the modern world. For an alternative and delightfully humorous primer on medieval Europe and the historical realities that surrounded it, see Ereira and Jones, *Medieval Lives*. See also Wells, *Barbarians to Angels*.

    2. It should be noted that the madness of the fanatical Enlightenment worship of human reason most greatly affected philosophy and science in its early years. However, during the time that Descartes was philosophizing, some rather significant progress was being made in the arts at the hands of masters who may not have come under the direct influence of rationalism, but who had, nonetheless, worked within the zeitgeist of the Enlightenment. As the Enlightenment sprang to life, Shakespeare was transforming the

Cogito Ergo Sum

Have you seen such men? In research laboratories they assemble, staring into microscopes and telescopes and claiming that though they have not yet explained—through materialistic assumptions—all the workings of the world, they will arrive if only given more time. They optimistically envision the wonders of the humanity of the future—enormous brains floating about, suspended by the sheer energy of their minds, gods of the universe. Others, however, pessimistically see themselves as a threat to the very world that pushed them from her womb and, in self-loathing, long for their own eradication. Have you seen such men whose intellectual certainty begins and ends within their own minds and will not be undone under any circumstance? They are the hallmark of all history. Nothing greater has yet been seen.

Insanity of insanities: The man who attempts to build complete certainty on his own fallible reason is insane. The skeptics were bad enough, but now this—now fallible man is made the source and judge of knowledge. Descartes' philosophical system attempted to place man at the center of the universe. Descartes was a rationalist, meaning that for him, reason took precedence over all other means by which knowledge may be acquired. The rationalist believes that reason is the road that leads to knowledge. Stay on the road and you will arrive at knowledge; trust your mind and the world of absolute knowledge will open wide before you. Even when you cannot trust your own perceptions of the world around you, you can at least rest confidently in the workings of your own noetic material.

For Descartes, the *cogito ergo sum* (I think, therefore, I am) was the foundation.[3] This was self-evident. It needed no explanation, no further proof, and no evidence. It was a basic belief that did not rely on any other belief or idea for its justification. It came to him ultimately by a form of *lumière naturelle*, or natural light.[4] Like an intuition impressed upon the mind, this lumière, this spontaneous impulse—unexplainable yet indubitable—drove Descartes to certainty. Though he gave no clear argument for

---

English language, Rembrandt was perfecting his painting technique, and J.S. Bach was composing works that flirted with musical flawlessness.

3. Our concern here is with Descartes' epistemic question: How can I be sure that I exist? This is not to say, however, that the metaphysical question of "being" or existence itself is of no import. Descartes had assumed that the concept of *being* was universal (clear) and self-evident, for which he was later criticized by Martin Heidegger. See Heidegger, *Being and Time* (various translations).

4 This is the *natural light* Descartes speaks of in the third meditation. Descartes, *Meditations*.

why he accepted the intuitions of natural light as a basis for certainty over and against the sensory experiences of the world around him, Descartes built his knowledge entirely on the basis of such mental phenomena. For Descartes, sensory-based experimentation could only "'suggest' truths that logic might later prove."[5]

The human mind, when salvaged from the weaknesses of the physical body, would no longer be susceptible to error. If left unhindered by the feeble and fallible flesh, this almighty mind could prove to be the foundation for certain knowledge. True irrationality—true madness—was a sickness brought on not by the mind, but by the physical substance of the brain that houses it. Human reason, if properly nurtured and disciplined, would save man from all his epistemic woes.

It must be understood that not all Enlightenment thinkers were rationalists. But though not all were rationalists, nearly all were committed to the idea that human effort would yield a bountiful intellectual harvest. But what of Descartes' rationalism? Had he submitted completely to the reason of man? Descartes' rationalism has been criticized because of its failure to live up to its name. He relied too heavily on natural light and intuition where he should have based his beliefs on a logical syllogism or mathematical truth. The "knowledge" that all thinking beings exist had been based on an assumption. Some philosophers have suggested that Descartes "smuggled" in a proposition that had not yet been demonstrated.[6] He had not adequately established that thinking was a necessary condition for existing. But despite this minor shortcoming, the Enlightenment project of human certainty that Descartes had introduced was now well under way, and there was no turning back from this new modern era.

This Enlightenment project was no mere trifle. The thinkers of the age were not simply engaged in fatuous competition for the most fanciful, mind-twisting notions or clever rebuttals to the counter-examples of their predecessors. The Enlightenment philosophers were driven by a thirst for knowledge that had become very dear to many of them. The autobiographical nature of Descartes' work shows us that his meditations were not abstract specimens of thought, to be labeled and shelved for later examination or displayed for the enjoyment of his guests. There was, rather, something very personal in these thoughts. Copleston suggests that Descartes "was animated, not by a merely superficial intellectual curiosity, but by a passion

---

5. Clark, *Thales to Dewey*, 249.
6. Ibid., 246.

for the attainment of certainty."[7] This passion would burn and spread to ignite the minds of others until, from the great furnace, true knowledge would be forged.

Baruch Spinoza was the second of the prominent rationalists of the seventeenth century. Having been influenced by Descartes, Spinoza sought to establish philosophical certainty by reason, but unlike Descartes, he reduced the entire universe to one substance: God. His reason led him to deny the existence of separate bodies and minds; in doing so he claimed that outside of God, no substance can exist, nor be conceived.[8] This pantheism, or belief that all things are God, was the logical result of his rationalism. For Spinoza, human knowledge was greatly affected by this pantheistic outlook intertwining the mind of God and man. Spinoza confidently stated that "the human mind is a part of the infinite intellect of God, and therefore, when we say that the human mind perceives this or that thing, we say nothing else than that God has this or that idea . . . ."[9] By making the mind of man into the mind of God, all the divine powers of knowledge were afforded a once feeble humankind.

For Spinoza, happiness, or contentment, was directly tied to knowledge of the mind of God. But as a pantheist, he had made man into something divine. His rationalism had made man the infallible source of all knowledge by attempting to give man the mind of God. Spinoza had wanted to elevate man to godhood, but succeeded only at emptying God of his epistemic power. Nothing had really changed in man except his self-confidence that he could go unaided into battle against skepticism and win. But while nothing had changed in man, everything had changed in God. Spinoza's God was so far removed from his biblical origins that no religious scholar would recognize him as the God of Scripture. By contrast, a biblical model of knowledge allows that God is all-knowing. In his omniscience, God knows the mind of man, thus knowing what man knows. But a biblical model of knowledge does not permit that man has full knowledge of the mind of God. These two remain separate.

Like Descartes before him, Spinoza's epistemology was grounded in the bold claims of human certainty. These bold claims of certainty were subsequently picked up by others, including G.W. Leibniz, a German philosopher and mathematician who emphasized the importance of *a priori*

---

7. Copleston, *Descartes to Leibniz*, 152.
8. Spinoza, "Ethic," 576.
9. Ibid., 594.

knowledge, this being knowledge gathered independently of sense-experience. Again, man was made the center of the universe, his throbbing seething mind the engine that would drive him. These titans of the philosophical world stop, therefore, at nothing to possess knowledge, perfect and pure.

The three mighty rationalists of the Enlightenment age (Descartes, Spinoza, and Leibniz) are known for their incredible minds and for the theories that still influence thinkers today. These were men whose quest for knowledge was not limited to philosophical inquiry, but also included explorations of physics, mathematics, and other sciences. Their influence spread from the continent of Europe to affect the work of the British empiricists—men like John Locke, George Berkeley, and David Hume. Based on the work of the rationalists, the empiricists began an investigation of knowledge by bowing to the primacy of experience. Like the rationalists, they were convinced that a proper inquiry into human knowledge would eliminate the meddling perturbations of skepticism. Even Hume was out for more than the paltry offerings of skepticism, which seemed to him a necessary counterbalance to the intellectual confidence of Locke and Berkeley. Certainty had been paramount for these men. In his *Essay Concerning Human Understanding*, Locke suggested that by a thorough exploration of the power of the human mind we shall not be led to the nagging repugnancy of doubt, nor to the intellectual idleness brought on by the prospect that knowledge may be unattainable.[10]

REASON'S LAST STEP

But is this confidence in the human mind an adequate cure for the infirmity of ignorance? Blaise Pascal, a contemporary of Descartes, was not convinced that the Enlightenment project would yield the intellectual certainty desired by these men. On a scrap of paper he had jotted the following note:

> Reason's last step is the recognition that there are an infinite number of things which are beyond it. It is merely feeble if it does not go as far as to realize that.[11]

Human reason has its limits. We are limited by the smallness of who we are. We are confined to the limits of our imagination. Even gazing though telescopes at the far reaches of the universe and seeing more clearly

---

10. Locke, *Essay Concerning Human Understanding*, 57–58.
11. Pascal, *Pensées*, 188/267; 56.

Cogito Ergo Sum

with each day the wonders of the "edges" of infinity, we are still bound to our limitations. We only ever look back . . . never forward. We create machines to store our "knowledge" for us—vast warehouses of data and information—but even these do not make us smarter. We have only displaced knowledge by equating it with mere data. The voluminous libraries of the world cannot implant the sum of their wisdom on our feeble minds. Each generation will repeat and rediscover that which has already been done in the area of learning. We come without knowledge into the world, and when we leave, we take the sum of our beliefs with us. We can leave information, but we cannot leave *justified true beliefs* for our children. These, they must develop for themselves from what we have given them. Knowledge is as fleeting as life itself, and the rational mind of man can do nothing to change this reality. At best, the rational mind is dismally impotent, misusing and exasperating reason by perpetually overdosing itself on its own stringent rationality. Are we truly any better off today than was the ignorant medieval peasant resting in his dusty hay field? Are we any better off than the troglodyte, sketching crude images on the stone of his cave by the light of his newly harnessed fire?

Let us look again at our first parents and that old creation story. We have seen how the biblical account of Adam and Eve's "skepticism" led to their fall, but what of their exploration of rationalism? One might say that Eve was the first epistemologist, after all. And having experimented with skepticism in the opening verses of Genesis chapter 3, she then tried her hand at epistemic certainty. Her doubts were first manifested against the serpent's cunning suggestions, then against her Lord and Creator.[12] These doubts edged her toward the abyss, but it was not her doubts that sent her tumbling. It was the enticing offer of *certainty* that led to her ultimate demise. The devil's offer was deliciously seductive. Eat the fruit and you will be like God, knowing good from evil (Gen. 3:5). Eat the fruit and you will have the mind of God, enlightened to the glorious beauty of a world that, until now, has been beyond your reach. Eat the fruit and all the epistemic powers of heaven will be yours. Knowledge, true knowledge, is what she craved. The physical qualities and sensuous appeal of the fruit were now

---

12. The image of the serpent is a rich metaphor intended to tell us something about Satan's character, not necessarily his appearance. Elsewhere in Scripture, he is described as a dragon that has been overcome by God (Rev. 20:2). In ancient literature, evil is often emblematized and personified as a serpent, a dragon, or a writhing sea beast. Scripture borrows this familiar metaphor but clearly depicts the covenant God of Israel as the triumphal conqueror of the beast through the salvific work of Christ (Gen. 3:15).

augmented by the mind-altering potion she believed it contained in its flesh. The decision was hers. Her ataractic husband would be of no help to her as she stood gazing, transfixed upon the fruit. The devil, fittingly described as a serpent, had made his case and now stood by like an unscrupulous merchant awaiting her decision. In the warmth and comfort of that paradise, she reached for the fruit and tasted it. Then she handed it to her complacent mate, who seems to have looked at it, shrugged, and taken a bite as well, offering neither counterargument nor any attempt at objection.

The fruit was there as a means by which God could test the faithfulness and love of his creation. This probational season was to serve as an opportunity for man to demonstrate that his moral freedom would lead him to God, not to self-love and pride. Yet, in reaching for that beautiful and horrible fruit, humanity's doom was sealed. As the forbidden fruit touched Eve's lips, her eyes were opened to a knowledge unlike anything she could have imagined. But something was not quite right. She was to have been like a goddess, peering down and into the world as through a microscope and gazing omnisciently at the principles of wisdom that only a god could understand. She was to have had knowledge like that of a physician who, studying the anatomy of the human body, understanding its workings, and diagnosing its sickness, would know far more than a common observer. But she was not a goddess, nor an omnipotent physician. She found that she was, instead, the diseased and dying patient, ignorant of the gravity of her own condition. Her knowledge of good and evil would come, not as one peering in from the outside, but as one afflicted with all the torment of evil while still desperately longing for good. Her knowledge of the universe would come not from transcendently gazing at its intricacy and beauty, but as one bound to its harsh uncaring momentum. Her knowledge of God would come, not from what she gained in walking with him in the cool of the morning, but in what she lost by her rebellion against him. Moreover, her knowledge of herself would be limited to the wretchedness of a fallen condition—one of weakness and sickness—removed from fellowship with God.

Skepticism alone leads to doubt. Reason alone leads to arrogance and false knowledge. Something more must govern what we know, but what? The blind forces of a godless universe have turned their wicked eyes upon us. Yet lacking both sight and insight, they only lead us to question if we are any better off today than in the age of Descartes or any other.

Cogito Ergo Sum

Of course, many would say we are. We have made great progress since the days of our first parents. We have gained knowledge never before imagined—knowledge of geology, biology, physics, mathematics, astronomy, and physiology. We have gazed into the beating heart of man. We have held the moon in our hands. We have built monuments to ourselves that point to nothing else but our greatness. And with all our knowledge swirling hectically around us, the university—that great center of learning—has attempted to bring order to the epistemic chaos that dominates the earth. But it too has failed.

We have claimed that man is the only source of knowledge. Man, like Atlas, is to hold upon his shoulders a great weight—the entirety of knowledge. Man will decide how knowledge is to be learned and applied, and in doing so, will move modern humanity out of the dark age. But this is absurd. Every age is dark. None is more enlightened than the others. When man is made the center and source of knowledge, he has bound himself ruthlessly to darkness. He becomes the center of the universe: the earth, moon, and stars revolving around him and bowing down before him in unrelenting worship.

The post-Enlightenment world suffers less now from roaming wolves, elves, and goblins but still endures the occasional torments of pest and disease. Witches are still at work mixing their brews, though the vocabulary has changed some. We might call them neo-pagans now. The wicked, mind-reducing dogmas of the church that once plagued Christendom have been replaced. Now behold the wicked mind-reducing dogmas of *scientism*, urging its adherents to uncritically embrace the doctrine of philosophical materialism and its denial of God.[13] The haymaker's kind has all but died out, but the "gamemaker" is still thriving. He sits, unthinking, in front of the lucent screen and fills his mind with bilge and drivel, soaking in all the diversions the information age has to offer. Further, the misplaced identities and gender confusion of the present age have made women into men and men into boys. A generation of young men too lazy to think, too lazy to work, and too lazy to see their own laziness has left the universities to women who are far more ambitious and capable than they. Even the universities grow tired of knowledge, and throw their dogmas and agendas like slop to the waiting ears of students.

---

13. Philosophical materialism is the doctrine that reality is made up of nothing but matter. It is an extreme form of empiricism that suggests that if you cannot experience it through your physical faculties then it cannot exist. This doctrine will be explored in further detail in the following chapter.

PART ONE: DESCENT INTO MADNESS

The days of sending our children to slave away in the fields, and later in the textile mills, has ended, but now we send them to abortion mills to be put to death before they have the opportunity to clutter an already over-cluttered world. Those who do live to see the light of day spend their early years in comfortable, well-lit, and well-furnished schools learning "useful" facts from teachers who teach them everything about nothing and nothing about who they are, what they are, or why they are. Black-souled scalawags issue from the most "civilized" of neighborhoods, fouling the earth with every conceivable perversion. But at least we have jet engines, espresso makers, and the world's news at our fingertips. Yes, I suppose we are comfortable and well-informed madmen, but madmen nonetheless.

It is clear that through our education we have become quite good at answering the questions of *how*, while neglecting the questions of *why*. How does one build a bridge? How does one cure a cancer? How does the universe work? We have asked these questions and even answered them in many ways. But we have not asked why. We have not explored the reasons and meaning that lead us to the "how questions." *Why* do we exist? *Why* is knowledge meaningful? Only when these questions are answered will we move forward upon a sure foundation and build a knowledge that endures. Knowing how something works is useless unless we also know why it works. Knowing how to sing means nothing if we do not know why we sing. Knowing how to love is useless unless we know why we love. Knowing how to acquire knowledge is futile if we know not why we value knowledge nor how knowledge serves us.

What have the philosophers taught us? How have they led us toward knowledge and cured us of our insanity? Only by demonstrating that unless we look to the all-knowing God, every attempt at knowledge will end in failure. Hume's epistemology only led him to some awkward place between knowledge and doubt. The last of the great empiricists, he had set forth his philosophy of doubt by questioning (as we have already briefly examined) the necessary connections between causes and their effects. Real knowledge is thus limited to the impressions that the world leaves upon us and to the ideas we have of those impressions. As we saw in chapter 2, this led Hume to criticize any ideas that require induction, such as the sun rose yesterday, the sun rose today, therefore the sun will rise tomorrow. What has happened in the past tells us nothing about what is happening today, so why bother with inferences? Why infer about tomorrow when tomorrow contains realities that may just be beyond our wildest imagination? And Hume's reply, "Don't bother."

More significant still, was Hume's belief that since human knowledge is limited to experience, it would be useless to argue for any kind of supreme being based simply on the observations man has made of the universe. For Hume it was absurd to think that observations of the physical realm might lead to conclusions about the spiritual world. If man were to deduce the existence of some kind of God based solely on his experiences, who knows what kinds of phantoms he would produce.[14] Hume demonstrated, therefore, that man's reason has some limit, but he also believed that man, through his inquiry into nature, would have to find knowledge by his own power, owing nothing to a supreme being. Man remained, for the empiricist, the measure of all knowledge.

Perhaps Hume's Enlightenment philosophy puts rationalism in its place, but even still, it does not offer a reliable source of knowledge. Limiting what is known to some few impressions does not leave us with a tenable worldview. Nor does the reduction of inflated intellectual pride offer us an alternative to the gnawing uncertainty that leaves us unable to answer the nagging questions of meaning, origins, and eternity. Hume believed that impressions and ideas of these impressions would have to suffice as the building blocks of any kind of knowledge, but where did Hume get the impression that knowledge is based on impressions?[15] His empiricism does little more than beg the question. Hume could not prove God's existence by the use of reason, but then again, he could not truly prove the existence of anything else for that matter. What he did establish, however, was the importance of his arguments to the ongoing debate in the field of epistemology.

This very brief synopsis of Enlightenment thought serves to establish one very important truth: A reliance on the mind of man produces mixed results. Human reason is necessary to establish a clear understanding of reality, truth, and knowledge. Likewise, human reason is necessary to understand reason's own limits. And these limits must also be acknowledged and appreciated, even if with sorrow and hesitation. One philosopher who did accept these limits (to some degree) was Immanuel Kant, who, after studying the work of Hume, was awakened from his "dogmatic slumber"

---

14. For more on Hume's critique of theistic arguments, see *Dialogues Concerning Natural Religion*.

15. Groothuis, "Questioning Hume's Theory," 32–33.

in order to participate in the humbling of reason. Kant's project was to fix limits for reason, and in so doing, prevent reason from trying to take knowledge where it should not go. Since he believed the world as we see it is understood through a combination of the impressions given by the senses and the ideas that the mind forces on us, he was concerned with eschewing the illusions that would begin to haunt and confound us if reason were to go beyond the senses. Our concepts of the world shape the world. And when these concepts are not properly constrained, we end up pushing our concepts beyond the realm of experience and into the world of chimeras, spooks, and goblins. Kant's desire was to fix limits to reason, that he might evade the world of metaphysical illusions while still avoiding the abyss of skepticism.

But this thinking only led Kant to a false modesty in reasoning, and the limitation of knowledge to things physically present. For Kant, man was still the rational god of the universe, the boundary setter, the creator of knowledge, and the definer of truth. Man was always the center of these philosophies—man with all his limits, man the fallible, man the reckless, man the insane. What Kant had proposed was a philosophy called *transcendental idealism*. Though it is difficult to understand exactly how Kant's complicated philosophy of idealism is to be taken, it may be suggested with all plausibility that under this system, the reality of the universe becomes dependent on man's interpretation of it. Truth is, therefore, made subjective.

Remember that knowledge has been defined by the *tripartite* analysis of *justified true belief*. As we have already seen, the project of skepticism is to attack justification by claiming that a true belief can never fully be defended against doubt. There is, however, another threat to knowledge. Rationalism and unthinking faith in reason can lead to a full-scale attack on reality or to an attack on our understanding of reality. In Kant's case, realities that are external to our minds, though they exist, become largely subjective and prone to skeptical attacks. We have already seen quite clearly that skepticism threatens the justification of beliefs. But not content to stop there, it continues its attack on knowledge in the form of anti-realism, and in so doing, threatens truth.

COMMON SENSE

When man becomes the center and source of knowledge, he binds himself to the subjectivity of his thoughts and of his interpretations of the reality around him. In essaying to find an adequate system of interpretation for his knowledge-claims, he is automatically led to suspicions concerning anything that does not conform properly to his system. Any clear sense about what is real and knowable is clouded by the very epistemic method that was intended to guarantee and preserve knowledge in the first place.

This is where good old-fashioned common sense can be dusted off and taken down from the shelf, for common sense has something to say to the skeptic as well as the rationalist. A little common sense epistemology will define terms with greater precision and guard meaning with greater care. We naturally get confused over truth when we try to define it epistemologically rather than metaphysically. What I mean is that truth does not depend on our epistemic certainty of it. The existence of a particular truth of reality is not dependent on my interpretation or justification of it for its validity. Truth is, rather, grounded in metaphysical objectivity. Truth is true insofar as it corresponds to reality. This is a metaphysical and not an epistemic claim. J.P. Moreland reasons that "reality makes thoughts true or false."[16] The content of a sentence is not made true by our belief in it or by our justification of it. Instead, "a proposition is true just in case it corresponds to reality, when what it asserts to be the case is the case."[17]

Reason alone, when uninterrupted by common sense, begins to demand epistemic certainty, and when it fails to find what it is looking for, retreats with frustration to skepticism by losing faith in knowledge. According to the common sense view of Thomas Reid, an eighteenth-century Scotsman well-versed in Hume, we must trust our knowledge-gaining faculties, for if we do not trust our own faculties and their ability to identify truth, then the whole project of philosophy is ruined. Everything we think and believe is based on the assumption that our capacity to know is not erroneous. It would do us some good if we asked ourselves this question a little more often: "If my reasoning results in conclusions that run contrary to everything that presents itself to me by common sense, only to end in absurdity, should I accept these results?" And if we are willing to ask this question, I hope we are equally willing to heartily answer, "No." *Common sense realism* allows us to make inferences that are perfectly reasonable and normal without having to offer infinite strings of proofs and indubitable

---

16. Moreland, "Truth," 78.
17. Ibid., 77.

foundations. Basic beliefs grounded in reality and common sense are foundational enough for building further and less justifiable beliefs.[18]

Cambridge philosopher G.E. Moore answered the challenge of skepticism, not with rationalist proofs but with a common sense approach similar to that of Reid. I find his argument far more rigorous and overwhelmingly convincing than any put forth by his predecessors.

> I can prove now, for instance, that two human hands exist. How? By holding up my two hands, and saying, as I make a certain gesture with the right hand, "Here is one hand," and adding, as I make a certain gesture with the left, "and here is another."[19]

Moore argued that his proof stands against scrutiny since it satisfies three important conditions. First, the conclusion that two human hands exist is not identical to the beginning premise, which is the visible gesticulations made by the hands. Second, the fact of the existence of the hands is known, and not simply believed or dreamed, by common sense. Third, the conclusion that two human hands exist flows logically from the premise that there are presently two human hands moving and gesticulating. Moore's conclusion: "It is perhaps impossible to give a better or more rigorous proof of anything whatever."[20]

Common sense reasoning, when undefiled by the excesses of Enlightenment extremes, can satisfy our need for knowledge by opening the doors to the storehouse of wisdom. When led by common sense and powered by the acceptance of reality as it stands, reason can lead us to gain knowledge about this world, and even gain access to metaphysical concepts and realities. I would advise these aforementioned merits of reason in opposition to Robert Fogelin's recent dreary suggestion that the intellectual activity of knowledge-gaining will inevitably lead to illusion or dissatisfaction.[21] In a way, he might be right, only insofar as man remains the source and end of reason. But if this is all there is to reason, and if reason cannot satisfy, why does Fogelin go on reasoning? His response: "It is often fun, and at best, high adventure."[22] For those who deny knowledge, and for those who

---

18. For a good defense of classical foundationalism that argues that every justified belief we have terminates in a foundation of basic beliefs, see G.E. Moore, "Defense of Classical Foundationalism."

19. Moore, "Defense of Common Sense," 53.

20. Ibid., 53.

21. Fogelin, *Walking the Tightrope*, 170.

22. Ibid., 170.

take fallible human reason too far, a satisfying knowledge will always be unattainable. "But so what," they say, "toying around with ideas sure is a hell-of-a-lot of fun."

Epistemology and the quest for knowledge can be fun (believe it or not), but the endeavors of reason account for much more than this. And though necessary, Fogelin's high adventure is not and should not be the ultimate. Our search is for the invaluable treasure of knowledge that is sure and livable. Reason gets us somewhere, but reason does not get us everywhere. On this simple point I can agree with Hume, with Kant, and with Fogelin. And on this same point I can agree with the words of the apostle Paul.

> Where is the wise man? Where is the scholar? Where is the philosopher of this age? Has not God made foolish the wisdom of the world? (1 Cor. 1:20)

Paul, in his first letter to the Corinthian church, is not trying to disparage learning, nor is he trying to slander knowledge and mock reason as a futile exploit. By offering a true *critique of pure reason*, he simply argues for the limits of human reason. Reason will lead a wanderer to many good places and shelter those who are weary from the storm of folly, but never will reason ultimately save a man's life. Even the foundations of knowledge that present themselves to us through common sense *a priori* truth claims are susceptible to skepticism or other epistemic attacks if these foundations are planted in a godless universe. Human reason has always been put forth as a means of salvation—salvation from boredom, salvation from meaninglessness, and salvation from moral chaos.[23] But one thing reason cannot save us from is its own nagging corruption. Paul reminds us that it is not human reason that leads man to God, but divine reason that leads God to man.

Redemption of the mind cannot come from the mind when the mind itself is corrupt. Paul goes on to say that since "the world through its wisdom did not know him, God was pleased through the foolishness of what

---

23. Several notable continental philosophers, including Luc Ferry and André Comte-Sponville, have continued this strain of thinking by proposing that philosophical reasoning alone is the only hope of salvation from the problem of meaninglessness. By presupposing the absurdity of a God-centered spirituality, they have posited instead, with obvious irony, a man-centered and spiritless spirituality. See Ferry, *Brief History of Thought*, and Ferry and Jerphagnon, *La tentation du christianisme*. See also Comte-Sponville, *L'Esprit de l'athéisme*.

was preached to save those who believe" (1 Cor. 1:21). And what was this foolishness, if nothing more than the simple truth that if we are to be saved from the doom of the corruption that extends even to the furthest faculties of our minds, we must look for a source outside ourselves. Reason must culminate in the self-illumination of its own inadequacy. And still, with reason at our side, we press on, searching for what we cannot find until the God of the universe reveals it in his good pleasure.

So where is the philosopher of this age? He is wandering about lost with the philosophers of every other age who have not let their reason be guided by something greater. The philosopher of this age is he who uses his reason but does so in the void.[24] His reason is not properly grounded, and he is driven insane because of it. Robert J. Gula begins his book *Nonsense* with this profoundly honest thought: "Are men and women by nature hopelessly muddled creatures? By nature, yes. Muddled, yes. Hopelessly, no."[25] Reason is something that is learned, and knowledge is something acquired. But again, where there is a muddled nature, hopelessness will always follow unless we find a hope outside ourselves.

My intention in this chapter is not (I assure you) to be too hard on reason, nor on the marvelous world of science that has done so much to drag our miserable carcasses out of the mire of intellectual fraud and inanity. Without reason we are doomed to mindlessness and perpetual stupidity, lacking the ability to observe, process, and enjoy our world. Without science we are fated with a drab and hopelessly intolerable world where nothing but mere subsistence is possible, and where hunched, unkempt men scratch about with bones in the dust. I do not damn reason nor do I deny that science will yield numerous marvels yet to be seen. But I do doubt that science will ever perfect or satisfy our reasoning. And this, I believe, is proved by the very claims of scientists who see themselves as the wellspring of certainty.

Cradled at the breast of reason and nursed on rational certainty and intellectual swell-headedness, we are not fully protected from the dangers that lurk in the epistemic shadows, for the shadow that casts the longest gloom is that of reason herself. She wears two faces, and we often see but one—that of an angel, soft-skinned and radiant. But when she turns her pretty face, we will see with horror a foul harpy bent on drugging us with her fetid sour rationalism. Unchecked, she would have us believe that

---

24. Chesterton, *Orthodoxy*, 22.
25. Gula, *Nonsense*, 2.

without her we would have nothing true and nothing justified. She leaves us to lust for her with such passion that our senses are dulled to the possibility that knowledge might be found elsewhere. But this too is madness. G.K Chesterton rightly observed that "the madman is not the man who has lost his reason. The madman is the man who has lost everything except his reason."[26] When our own reason becomes our god, we have nowhere else to turn but inward. And while the ancient troglodyte built his god from stone, we have made ours from our own minds, and worshiped it with the same knowledge-corroding vulgarity. Yes, we are insane.

26. Chesterton, *Orthodoxy*, 13.

5

Philosopher of This Age

"Tomfoolery!" exclaimed the pedantic professor, leaning back in his chair and raising one eyebrow as if tipping his hat to reason. "Yes, yes, blatherskite indeed," agreed his exasperated colleague, the morning sun reflecting in his untidy hair and forming an aura of glory around his magnificent brain-brimming cranium. These men had long battled against intellectual impropriety and had the scars to show for it: an ink spot under the left breast pocket, mismatched socks, a tobacco pipe, a well-groomed beard, a tweed jacket, a stack of ungraded papers, brown loafers. They had done battle with fountain pens and rhetoric and had fought the good fight against . . . hogwash.

The world has seen enough nonsense, has it not? Contradiction, convolution, and congestion of the mind are a scourge to be reckoned with. Our impressionable minds fall frequently ill with unjustified non-truths, but no medicine seems to remedy the problem of poppycock.

Do not for a moment forget about our shared condition of madness. We take our insanity with sugar and cream. Arsenic tastes better that way. The poisonous beliefs we swallow scream and sear through our minds, numbing us to the uncomfortable realities we wish to avoid. This is why beliefs often reflect what we want—and what we want is to scald our senses to the irritating reality that we are *not* the center of the universe, the means-and-end of knowledge. We want to be gods who judge the actions of our unthinking mother—she being the universe. But how has this improved us? The medieval man thought himself the center of the universe because

God had made it so; the enlightened modern man thinks himself the center of the universe because he has made it so; both are equally satisfied with themselves and both are equally insane. Or are they? The enlightened modern man wields a weapon of great power: reason. Unlike the feudal peasant floundering in ignorance, or the superstitious Christian who has apparently denied all reason, the progressive philosopher of this age has supposedly obtained objectivity of thought, knowledge of science, and the ability to think freely and originally.

Enraged by thousands of years of unchecked nonsense, some few courageous men and women have finally taken it upon themselves to cleanse the world of its epistemic sins. They have assured us that knowledge will be achieved if only we look in the right places while using the right methods. And what are the right places? *Man and his brain.* What are the right methods? *Philosophical materialism and its God-evading explanation of reality.*

MATERIALISTIC BELIEFS

We briefly encountered philosophical materialism in the last chapter. In this view, material objects are the only things that exist in the universe. Material objects are the only things that can be known. This extreme form of empiricism takes issue with the existence of anything that cannot be measured by science and its method. For this reason, materialism denies God while acknowledging religion only as a mental phenomenon explainable through biological research or sociological study. One famous proponent of materialism, Bertrand Russell, proselytized that man, his origin, his character, and his knowledge "are but the outcome of accidental collocations of atoms."[1] The fundamental materialistic doctrines are, as he went on to argue, so nearly certain "that no philosophy which rejects them can hope to stand."[2] The blind unthinking universe has given birth to a very complex material creature: man.

So intellectually prodigious is this meat-machine (man), and so strange and unfathomable the workings of his mind, that entire branches of science and philosophy are dedicated to understanding him. And ironically, the entire scientific project of assessing nature depends on *him*—man, the product of nature. Yes, he is a god unto himself—incubated in the womb of his cold uncaring cosmos-of-a-mother, birthed in the black of

1. Russell, "Free Man's Worship," 314.
2. Ibid., 314.

the universe, devoured and synthesized in her grinding jaws, and digested into the dust that will form him anew. The innumerable writings of evolutionary biologists constitute our new sacred texts. The old creation myths have been reworked and reconstructed by materialism so as to form a new canonized doctrine.[3]

That ancient, scheming, lightning-bolt tyrant of a dimple-cheeked old man is best left seated on his cotton-candy-clouded throne, in a painting, in a museum, out of sight. God does not exist, and since God does not exist, argues Daniel Dennett (a leading proponent for materialism), belief in God can and should be explained as a natural phenomenon. It would follow, then, that if such belief can be explained as a natural phenomenon, there is no need to think that God exists.[4] In this argument, Dennett commits a surprisingly large amount of time and energy to a polemic that chases its own tail— revealing an underlying faith in and devotion to *scientism*, which is itself a religion of radical empiricism. If you cannot touch it, see it, measure it, poke it, or prod it, then it most certainly does not and cannot exist. Given this assumption, the philosophical materialist has nowhere else to look but to himself and to his own reason for answers to life's ultimate questions.

But where else could infinite knowledge be hidden, asks the philosophical materialist, than in man's mind, where it has been tucked safely away to be used by this enlightened generation? The materialist with his atheistic assumptions does not hesitate to receive human reason as an object of worship. Bowing in humble worship before the mirror, Emma Goldman asserted that "atheism in its negation of gods is at the same time the strongest affirmation of man."[5] For the materialist, a universe free from the perturbations of belief in God is a universe where the accolade to belief in man can be freely and joyously exercised. In such a universe, scientific inquiry can be generously executed in the peaceful quiet of reason without

---

3. Many scientists of materialistic leanings have suggested that they would gladly discard their materialism in favor of other more valid theories if only suitable alternatives could be discovered. Unfortunately, these same men and women refuse to examine any evidence that would usurp their assumptions, taking instead the position of Russell and claiming dogmatically that no alternative to materialism can hope to stand. This attitude is, however, destructive to the scientific method.

4. See Dennett, *Breaking the Spell*. In the opening pages of his book, Dennett wastes no time in stating that science has a privileged view of the world, and that belief in God is little more than a cognitive function to be studied.

5. Goldman, "Philosophy of Atheism," 133.

subjection to the anxieties of ignorant clergy that had once come seething and pouting into every conversation.

The radical empiricism of philosophical materialism was vehemently defended by A.J. Ayer, who criticized as absurd the idea that knowledge could ever introduce us to a "reality transcending the world of science and common sense."[6] For Ayer, not only was it absurd to suggest that knowledge of God is possible, it was equally absurd to make any theological assertions whatsoever about God. Ayer's materialism denied him knowledge of anything he could not see and, like David Hume, did not afford him the capacity to reflect on the nature of God or the possibility that God himself is responsible for human knowledge. The epistemologist who stepped beyond the empirical world was thought to have taken one step too far. And with this ambitious epistemologist in mind, Ayer posed this question:

> What valid process of reasoning can possibly lead him [the epistemologist] to the concept of a transcendent reality? Surely from empirical premises nothing whatsoever concerning the properties, or even the existence, of anything super-empirical can legitimately be inferred.[7]

According to Ayer's reasoning, the beginning and end of knowledge is to rest in the control of mortal man—the epistemic alpha and omega.

It is a troubling thought that squabbling, fallible philosophers bear the burden of determining what we know and how we know it, especially when these philosophers dwell in the same epistemic camp as Ayer, Dennett, and Russell. Our despair at this prospect is in the fact that—as we will soon see—radical empiricism leads only to skepticism. Surely Ayer was insane.

But we are all insane, and at times, even the most pious theists have joined in to sing the praises of man-the-infallible while making the unchanging God subject to the latest and most fashionable trends of human reason. Even among the most devout theists, man has become the center. It is no surprise, then, that a number of modern day atheists—self-ascribed worshipers of human reason and practitioners of materialistic

---

6. Ayer, "Verification Method," 469. Ayer subscribed to a belief system known as logical positivism, which saw particular success in the early and mid-twentieth century. Positivism was an ultimate failure because it was shown that its own principle empirical verification could not be empirically verified. For example, the statement, "a thing must be verified by observation to be true," is not verifiable since it is an abstract statement and has no physical qualities.

7. Ibid., 469.

assumptions—have argued that *real* knowledge is forfeited when man succumbs to theistic belief.[8] *Real* knowledge is said to be reasonable and godless. Knowledge, it is thought, is the logical conclusion of man's everyday cognitive functions, which have been knit together by countless ages of blind organic composition. If nothing else, man at least functions according to his physical construction as it was brought into being by the unremitting and violent forces of nature. The idea of man's function is essential to our conversation, and I would suggest that it is on the question of function that the materialist's argument perilously wobbles.

WHEN THE MIND FUNCTIONS PROPERLY

The fact that human beings function is undeniable. We are reminded of this when standing in a crowded market with hordes of desperate *functioners* bustling and stampeding about in search of the best products at the cheapest prices. We are reminded of this when listening to a convincing argument delivered by an orator who functions with great rhetorical skills. We are reminded of our functionality when met with the reality that, on a basic level, people do nothing other than function. Our function is to move about, to consume, to perform various actions, to think, and to pass our hereditary material into subsequent generations. It is unlikely that any materialist would doubt that human beings function. But if the materialist devoutly clings to his materialistic presuppositions and faith in human reason and goes on to live consistently with his materialism, he must not mistakenly think that humans function *properly*.

No, from his materialistic viewpoint, human beings do not function properly, for this assumes that they are *designed* for a specific function, and the materialist already assumes that there is no grand cosmic designer. Nor do human beings malfunction, for this assumes that they have failed to do what it is they were designed to do. For the materialist, there is no possibility of good function, bad function, proper function, malfunction, dysfunction, or the like. There are really only two possibilities for man in a materialistic universe: to function or not to function.

Alvin Plantinga, who developed this idea in great detail, points out that a universe devoid of God "cannot accommodate the idea of *proper*

---

8. It must be noted that not all atheists are materialists. There are some who subscribe to metaphysical dualism.

function."[9] Living creatures in such a system could never function properly because they would possess no designed plan or purpose that requires right belief or action. Health, sickness, sanity, or insanity would be meaningless linguistic clutter for the materialist.[10] Plantinga goes on to say that "the notion of proper function really applies only to things that have been designed by conscious, purposeful intelligent agents."[11] A clock functions properly only when all the components operate according to the design purpose of the clockmaker.

William Lane Craig and J.P. Moreland add that this proper function is to be understood as normative, meaning that proper function must not be defined by its *statistical* performance but on how it ought to function were it to function *correctly*.[12] After all, it is possible for a majority of clocks to consistently keep the wrong time because of malfunction, in which case the statistically normal clock would be one that does not work well. Likewise, it is possible (and quite likely) for a majority of people to be hopelessly insane according to the criteria presented in the first chapter. In this case, the statistically normal person would be the one who is unable to process information correctly and whose cognitive faculties produce untrue beliefs and entice him to destructive behavior.

Put simply, the argument is this: In order to have knowledge, it must be shown that the mind of the knower is functioning properly, in which case he would be justified or warranted in his belief. Without the guarantee of proper function, he would be without the guarantee of solid justification for his beliefs and would be condemned to a life of skepticism. The only assurance, therefore, of proper function and thus, knowledge, is the existence of a designer who has put in place all the cognitive components conducive to knowledge production.[13]

Man's great faith in his own reason cannot be accommodated in a materialistic universe. At best, the most erudite of rationalists, and the most

---

9. Plantinga and Tooley, *Knowledge of God*, 19.

10. Ibid., 19.

11. Ibid., 20. Plantinga also acknowledges that there are some nuances to his explanation of proper function. A refrigerator that has been designed to keep things cool can malfunction in that it begins to heat items, in which case it may now be thought to be functioning properly as an electric heater. However, he suggests that proper function must still be explained in terms of a designer. For a treatment of these issues, see Plantinga, *Warrant and Proper Function*, particularly 21–31.

12. Craig and Moreland, *Philosophical Foundations*, 103.

13. Ibid., 104.

scholarly of empiricists, are doomed to doubt the reliability of their own belief-producing faculties. As they concoct beliefs in the laboratories of their brains, the agonizing side effects of foundationless knowledge-claims will surge like venom through their doubt-stricken minds. This is certainly the case today. Behind the doors of this chemist's lab a great commotion now rages, and what emerges when the sparks cease and smoke clears is a madman who believes knowledge possible but whose worldview is unable to accommodate it.

To this, the philosophical materialist would likely retort that his unguided evolutionary processes could ultimately yield a crop of organic hominid apparatuses capable of possessing justified true beliefs. After all, an organism would be more likely to survive were it able to develop knowledge and use that knowledge to give it advantage in its fight for survival. *Knowing* where to hide, when to strike, what to avoid, and how to find food would give any creature some advantage over those who simply function according to genetic programming. Evolution favors those who can adapt to their environment.

Is not knowledge man's means of adaptation? Perhaps it is. But remember that the humanity of the materialist does not possess *properly* functioning cognitive faculties. The meat-machine we call man possesses *merely* functioning cognitive faculties, but nothing more. If there is no source—no God—behind his knowledge-building material, then man is left to trust his beliefs to a blind evolutionary process—a process that could produce "beliefs that have no causal relationship whatever to behaviors and thus no purpose or function."[14]

Unguided evolution could produce behaviors that are conducive to survival while allowing the organism to possess superfluous beliefs that have no bearing on the behavior of the organism. He could possess beliefs that neither cause behaviors nor result from behaviors. Furthermore, even if unguided evolution produced beliefs, these could be the effects of behavior but not the causes of behavior. They would be like fleeting dreams that wisp away in the light of morning and have no bearing on the behaviors of the individual. As Craig and Moreland point out, such beliefs would be mere decorations, having nothing to do with the survival of an organism.[15]

Though it may be possible for unguided evolutionary processes to produce behaviors that both cause and are caused by beliefs, Plantinga

14. Ibid., 103.
15. Ibid., 104.

argues that such beliefs would not necessarily have truth as their goal, nor would they be justified.[16] Man could adapt a behavior that allows him to avoid poisonous mushrooms even though he believes that what he actually sees are stinging hedgehogs or animal droppings.

It should not be thought that the possession of rational faculties—aptitudes that lead toward the possibility of gaining knowledge—is advantageous in a materialistic view of reality. After all, the development of the sophisticated cognitive capacities of a human being require a tremendous gestational period and a lengthy period of complete vulnerability before the human child is capable of sustaining itself in the hostile world. Knowledge-producing capacities pose a risk to human life from start to finish. What evolutionary advantage could possibly be found in knowledge and the misery that comes with it? The earthworm is all too happy in its stupidity. But even if some advantage could be found for us, we would not be guaranteed freedom from maladaptive cognitive functions or from the problem of skepticism.

Nature is concerned neither with justification nor with truth. The genes that she produces are interested only in man getting food into his mouth to give him the energy required to find a mate, copulate, and produce offspring. Belief is secondary, if not meaningless. Nature does not care what man believes or whether appearances are illusory. Both sanity and insanity would be impossible in such a universe, replaced with cognitive neutrality.

To this, our dear materialistic professors would object, suggesting that our proper function is quite possibly verified by simply comparing our function to the previous generation. Our fathers and mothers developed beliefs about the universe, as did their parents and their grandparents before them. Since these beliefs served them well enough to keep the race alive, we might assume that our ancestors not only functioned, but functioned properly. Why assume that we have nothing to which we may compare ourselves? We could reason that an organism has proper function if it is a reproduction of a previous organism that functioned in the same way. If the current organism exists, it is because its ancestor did its job well.

Unfortunately, this solution requires properly functioning ancestors. But are we truly justified in believing that the genes of our predecessors are free from malfunction? The answer to this is a resounding "No!" If only Pyrrho were here now. What would he say? With disappointment in his

---

16. See Plantinga, *Warrant and Proper Function*, chapters 1 and 2.

face, he would likely shake his head and scold us by retorting, "How do you even *know* that you have any ancestors, let alone the fact that they functioned correctly?"

Imagine a mutation introduced into the human population. A brilliant madman, in the deep pits of his secret laboratory, has mixed a potion that is released into the world. As it scalds and spoils its way through the population, very few are left untouched by its effects. It is a poison so destructive that it makes ears fall off and limbs contort. It dulls the minds of its victims and makes those affected unable to speak or communicate. Now, generations later, nothing has changed. A large majority are seen by the few unaffected as little more than crook-shanked mutes. Yet, despite their mutations, they still possess enough human qualities to be considered human. What then? Do these people function properly? The materialist may reply that yes, they do function properly given the numerous generations that validate their normality. But if proper function becomes relative to the majority that defines it, we are again left with the question of what really constitutes proper function. Malfunction can become proper function and proper function, malfunction. This gets us nowhere but back to the same old inability to suggest that there is any real difference between good function, bad function, proper function, malfunction, dysfunction, sanity, insanity, or the like.

With no designer in place to ensure the proper function of an organism, in an environment conducive to knowledge-gaining, there is little to justify beliefs in a purely material universe.[17] We may only find ourselves as hopelessly lost in the labyrinth of skepticism as ever before. If we cannot trust the functionality of our noetic equipment, there is no place left for us than at the feet of our master, Pyrrho. Skepticism is the logical result of materialism. Knowledge is not possible in a godless universe because justification for the truth of beliefs is not possible in a godless universe.

THE DENIAL OF BELIEF

The Enlightenment project had brought godless reason to men, only to make godless men unreasonable. Unsatisfied with Descartes' rationalism, the empiricists attempted to counter with arguments built upon man's relationship to the observable world—a world that excludes the supernatural.

---

17. Plantinga lays out this argument in great detail in *Warranted Christian Belief*.

Philosopher of This Age

In this view, immaterial beliefs are said to be of a fictitious realm—unfathomable, unbeknownst, and unacceptable to the materialist.

The irony here is too much, I'm afraid. The materialist believes that the bygone days of a spirit-haunted world teeming with ghosts, ghouls, and gods is long over. The age of the rationalist and of the radical empiricist is at hand. The age of the *reasonist* is upon us. A new order will rise from the invisible ashes of the spirit realm, and the intellectual exploits of humanity will be governed by the iron mind of the materialist. But back to the irony. The materialist has dismissed the prospect of an immaterial mind and all that goes with it. But in doing so, he forces himself into the absurdity of either abandoning belief all together or embracing a contradiction. After all, the materialistic belief that immaterial objects do not exist is itself immaterial. Last I checked, beliefs could not be squeezed, poked, jabbed, boiled, or preserved in ice. It is, therefore, unfortunate for the materialist that neither our beliefs nor our relationships to these beliefs can be accounted for. As Plantinga points out, the logical conclusion of a worldview that denies the existence of anything immaterial is the denial of belief itself.[18] And without belief, there can be no knowledge.

Transforming beliefs into something physical will not do. Man is more than a material cognition machine. Yes, a physical brain is necessary to human knowledge. But as Raymond Tallis asserts, "While to live a human life requires having a brain in some kind of working order, it does not follow from this fact that to live a human life is to *be* a brain in some kind of working order."[19] Knowledge is more than the result of chemical reactions and other physical phenomena bumping about in our heads. Tallis argues that while materialism can explain certain neural activities that account for our perception of objects, it offers nothing in the way of an explanation for intentionality or "the way that we are conscious *of* something."[20] Likewise, materialism offers no account for how the content of our reflections are *about* things or how such thoughts are focused on things other than ourselves.[21]

For instance, if you were to look at a large billboard adorned with a picture of Friedrich Nietzsche and the words, "God is dead," certain neurological activities would result. From a purely physical perspective, light

18. Plantinga and Tooley, *Knowledge of God*, 68.
19. Tallis, "What Neuroscience Cannot Tell Us," 4.
20. Ibid., 8.
21. Ibid., 8.

would reflect from the image of Nietzsche and onto your visual pathways, creating perceptions of the billboard to be stored as memories. But though the materialist may be able to explain *how* we see an object, he cannot explain *why* we perceive the object and accept it as something other than, and outside of, ourselves. Our reflections on the appearance of Nietzsche's profile and his famous aphorism are simply unexplainable to the materialist. Moreover, any thoughts on the content of what was perceived, which would develop into beliefs, would be equally unexplainable.

Some proponents of materialism willingly accept the consequences of their philosophical outlook. As a radical empiricist, philosopher Alex Rosenberg is disposed to deny intentionality by saying "that one clump of matter can't be *about* another clump of matter."[22] In other words, human matter cannot think about or hold beliefs about other matter. Consequently, humans cannot possess knowledge since knowledge requires both thinking and belief about various things. In denying *aboutness*, materialists cannot think about anything, even their own materialism. Ironically, Rosenberg's materialism must be false if we are to hold any kind of belief *about* it. Furthermore, Nietzsche's statement about the absence of a nonmaterial God means nothing unless we can grant the existence of nonmaterial realities, including God.

G.W. Leibniz understood this when he argued that reasoning, reflecting, and thinking in general cannot arise from pure material interactions. If a simple quark or electron cannot think or believe, then neither could an atom possess this ability. Further, if an atom is unable to think or believe, then why should we think that a molecule, a cell, or an organ could arrive at successfully surmounting this impossibility?[23] While Leibniz's argument is not conclusive, his point should be well taken: *The sum of material substance should not be thought to contain any more rationality than the parts.* A material brain could no doubt process the information received upon looking at the billboard, but only an nonmaterial mind could muster the epistemic fortitude to say, "Hold on there Mr. Nietzsche, I beg to differ."

The materialist cannot concede the reality of (nonmaterial) mental states. All that is left is our interpretation of that which impresses itself on our brains. But here, there are no facts or justified true beliefs—only interpretations of that which happens around us. These interpretations are

---

22. Rosenberg, *Atheist's Guide to Reality*, 186.
23. Plantinga and Tooley, *Knowledge of God*, 53.

subject to further interpretation with no end in sight and no possibility of ever knowing reality.[24]

And so, as the argument goes, materialism cannot account for properly functioning cognitive apparatuses or for beliefs. The radical empiricist is no more likely to escape his insanity than the rest of us who have thus far tried and failed miserably. But what if the materialist simply shrugs and denies the existence of belief? What if he replaces belief with some kind of epistemologically meaningless physical phenomena ignited in the brain by purely natural forces? Certainly, such explanation would lock any discourse on the subject into a stalemate because all "beliefs" (mental states) on the question would be preprogrammed by the physical matter and natural environment of the thinker. This would render his opinions unmovable from their preprogrammed standing. In this view, we would have absolutely no physical capacity to deviate from our beliefs no matter how strong the evidence against them.

Furthermore, only a madman who suffers a worse insanity than our own would suggest with a straight face that beliefs are impossible. You have thousands of beliefs swirling about in your mind at this very instant. You have already made up your mind about things you like and dislike. You have arrived at certain beliefs concerning the validity of the arguments presented above. And it is certain that your beliefs have led you to embrace a variety of hopes and desires for your future, both near and distant. If human insanity has reached the point of denying the existence of beliefs, then there is little hope left for us. In this case we may be left to go about our important work of shoveling the moon's reflection out of the water, building walls around trees so that they do not run off, or whatever else it is that occupies our loony time. But as for me, I should hope that I have not yet fallen quite that far into madness.

Between our malfunctioning intellect and perfectly healthy ignorance, we think that commitment to human reason will lead the honest, rational, thinking man away from belief in God. On the contrary, commitment to human reason leads to nowhere but skepticism. Only when God designs the cognitive material and instills proper function can knowledge happen. If anyone is so bold as to suggest that knowledge exists, his claim must be accompanied by belief in God.

However, belief in God is troublesome for many because if we are forced to accept God's existence for the sake of knowledge, then we are

24. See Smith, *Naturalism and our Knowledge*.

equally forced to live as if there is a God and accept the implications of such. And nobody wants to deal with the nonsense that goes along with theistic belief—throwing virgins into volcanoes, flagellating ourselves, and abstaining from sex forever because it is evil. Is there no possibility of somehow retaining knowledge while discarding the divine villain at its source? The answer to this is a simple no. As we will see in the coming chapters, the all-knowing "villain" who lies at the source of all human knowledge is not really villainous at all. If you want to make any knowledge-claim whatsoever, God is a necessary condition to that claim.

As we have seen, the materialist's conviction that justified true beliefs are possible in his god-forsaken universe requires the intellectual dexterity of a professional conjurer. To produce a believable illusion of the possibility of knowledge is not the work of the cheap epistemic trickster, but of a grand illusionist. Sadly enough, for the radical empiricist, professional conjurers are difficult to come by. And when illusionists cannot be found, we must settle for the next best thing: philosophers.

Where then is the philosopher of this age? Where is the wise man? I think the apostle Paul's question still retains its validity (1 Cor. 1:18–31). Human wisdom leads to many great discoveries, but it can never explain itself. An explanation of our capacity to possess knowledge can only come from God.

"But I object to this divine drivel," cries the professor, whose petulant self-confidence remains untouched. "We *reasonists* have discredited the medieval delusions of anything supernatural." Indeed, our professor is correct. He has fought relentlessly to discredit the outrageous supernatural story of a God who made man with the extraordinary ability to think. Our beloved professor has crafted a man whose knowledge-building capacities simply sprang into existence in the deep alchemist's pits of the unthinking earth. But as G.K. Chesterton argues, our dear professor has discredited "supernatural stories that have some foundation, simply by telling natural stories that have no foundation."[25] When the root is destroyed, the tree is sure to topple.

Richard Dawkins—biologist, intellectual, professor, and madman—has said that, in reality, we are all atheists.[26] There are gods out there in which we all refuse to believe. Dawkins is, no doubt, correct to some extent. But it may be more accurately said that in reality we are all theists. As we

25. Chesterton, *Orthodoxy*, 40.
26. See Dawkins, *Devil's Chaplain*, 150.

have seen above, we must assume the existence of God if we are to assume any other knowledge whatsoever. This assumption is itself the foundation on which Dawkins stands in order to make his god-denying claim.

Concerning the nature and scope of epistemic inquiry, the Enlightenment project has led to some rather false conclusions. Among them is the idea that the eternal, omniscient, omnipotent, and omnipresent God of Christianity can be studied in a biologist's laboratory along with all the other living organisms of the natural world. "We would gladly believe in a divine spirit," concur the radical empiricists, "if only some physical evidence could be put forth." But in presupposing the impossibility of the existence of a spiritual being, they have already reached their conclusion of unabashed denial of God, even before the slightest hint of an argument to the contrary can be mustered.

Belief in God has long been said to appeal only to those who carry with them some unrelenting fear of the world—fear of death, fear of abandonment, fear of the dark-night-of-not-knowing. It has been said that the Christian is he who desperately needs the assurance that there is a God out there who will protect him from everything not yet explained by science. It is said that Christianity, and its God, are for those who are afraid of the dark. But as Oxford mathematician John Lennox retorts, "Atheism is for those who are afraid of the light."[27] The true light of knowledge can come only from God himself.

The Enlightenment promise of certain knowledge has failed. Descartes' meticulous reasoning was not immune to the critique that followed. Others came after, presenting their epistemologies and demonstrating that justified true belief would be possible if only their systems and definitions were strictly kept. But all they proved was that whenever man is placed at the center of knowledge, little epistemic work is accomplished. Monoliths in our honor are built only to be torn down by subsequent generations. Ideas are designed, remodeled, reconstructed, or simply left to crumble by the corrosion of neglect. The philosopher of this age has left nothing lasting.

Philosophy, as a discipline, has always been concerned with the basic search for meaning. But when we hold beliefs that we alone justify, and that we alone make true, we make meaning meaningless. Meaning shifts like shadows, subject to the moods and whims of temperamentally mercurial

---

27. Though this statement, unbeknownst to me, may be recorded in one of his works, I heard Dr. Lennox make this clever aphorism in a lecture he gave at Westminster Chapel in London in the autumn of 2011.

people—here one day and gone the next. This is the greatest insanity of all. We have all seen the fruit of the madman's labors. He does not know who or what he is, and so he does not know how to affirm either his life or the lives of others. He *knows* we are little more than nothing in a cold, uncaring world, and so he cares nothing for man. Yet he *knows* that love, justice, liberty, and human rights for all are virtues to be kept. Ask him how he *knows* this. He knows because something in him makes him believe it and fight for it with all his being. He *knows*, but he does so without truth and without justification. He affirms man and denies him at the same time. His knowledge is empty. The madman—the philosopher of this age—will chase his own tail into the next age where another degenerate generation of geniuses will do the same. Let us not forget that even the latest cutting-edge insanity is insanity nonetheless. But what does the madman care?

The skeptic fears knowledge and the lover of reason is obsessed with knowledge, but in reality both of them hate knowledge with all their heart, mind, and soul. The skeptic is running away from knowledge because he fears what he may learn. He hates knowledge because he hates the God who alone can bring certainty to an uncertain world. He does not want to know because he does not want to be known. In much the same way, he who is devoted to human reason is infatuated with knowledge, not because he loves it but because he wishes for complete control over it, refusing to let it guide him. He wants knowledge of both God and man, but by making man into God, he ends up knowing neither. He wants to be alone in the universe, and with arms flailing and legs kicking, he drives the true source of knowledge as far from him as he can.

We may all have a little insanity in us, but the skeptic and the lover of human reason have the worst of it. These *brights*, these temperate intellectuals, these life-affirming believers in the goodness of humanity, brimming with love for mankind and hope for the future, are ready to tear the theist limb from limb simply because he has a supernatural foundation for the truth claims he believes.[28] You cannot deny God and love knowledge, because to deny God is to hate the very Source of knowledge. This is indubitable.

We who remain in our insanity and revile God's common grace do not properly know God, and since we do not properly know God, we lack the

---

28. The term *bright*, or *brights* in its plural form, has been employed by some as a substitute for negative charged terms like atheist or non-believer. But I say that unless God stops existing (a logical impossibility) there will hardly be anything bright about denying him.

ability to know ourselves, ultimately misplacing ourselves in the creation order. Once misplaced, we can undermine our importance, and thus undermine the severity of our rebellion against God. If we are only animals, mere products of nature, simple beasts trying to do our best to make our world a better place, then we will justify (as we have for millennia) every kind of atrocity imaginable. We will attain the fullness of our insanity and self-destruct. By failing to know God, we can invite insufficiencies into our moral reasoning that result in a calamitous view of God's creation. That which is important to God is made trivial to us, and the hierarchy of created things becomes muddled and unsure. Man, the paramount of God's creation, loses his crown and becomes indistinguishable from any other living things. Our ignorance of God incites the blatant ignorance of God's image in man, allowing us to dismiss human intrinsic value, and in doing so, dismiss humanity. It troubles us naught to take a human life when the value of that life is indistinguishable from that of a slime mold.

As one would expect in a society driven by philosophical materialism and Darwinism, the weakest are the first to go. This means the very young and the very old are among the first to suffer at our hands. Abortion mills are in full operation in many countries where executioners in the guise of doctors offer to destroy human life with the blessing of both citizens and governments alike. When we lose our knowledge of what human beings are (image-bearers of God who enjoy intrinsic value) and why human beings exist (to glorify God), our insanity drives us to the most strange, abnormal, and dare I say, sinful behaviors. In adjacent hospital rooms, one team of doctors and nurses may be struggling to save the life of a premature infant, while another team works to brutally murder a child for no reason but that of being conceived at an inopportune time.

This is nothing new. Madmen have been justifying and facilitating the destruction of life for centuries. Perhaps we think that by destroying human beings—*image*-bearers of God—we can destroy God himself. Our minds are sick with insanity; our intellects thrash about uncontrollably; we hate God and want to be God all at once. And so we exercise our sovereignty over our world. The unborn must be stopped before they usurp us, the aged must be destroyed before they remind us of our mortality, and those who do not mirror our vision of what man should be must face annihilation before their existence proves that we are but mere humans and not gods at all.[29]

29. Some madmen have gone so far as to argue that it is always wrong to bring new

PART ONE: DESCENT INTO MADNESS

Much ink has been spilled thus far in bringing us to the simple conclusion that a skeptical approach to knowledge is not livable, and that reliance on human reason is not tenable. Despite all my ranting, I am by no means suggesting that our professors cap their fountain pens, shave their beards, and close their books like lids on coffins. What I am suggesting is that we allow ourselves the possibility, the probability, the (dare I say) certainty that God is the source of knowledge, and that only an epistemology that allows for his existence will achieve practical, believable, and satisfying results. As we have seen, knowledge that comes from within us is weakened by our limitations and failures. Knowledge must, therefore, come from something outside of us, namely God. And this God must not simply be some mere superhuman of the Greek myths or just any conceivably great thing. We are not talking about fairies, hobgoblins, or flying spaghetti monsters, but about a God who is perfect in being and whose power extends to his omniscience, that is, his capacity to know all things.

Only a being of perfect knowledge could serve as a source for our own. Only a being of perfect knowledge could guarantee human knowledge that is justifiable and trustworthy. Only a being of perfect knowledge could provide a reality in which truth is possible. It is under the lordship of God alone that belief is substantiated and validated. A lesser god than this will not do because a lesser god will be prone to the same errors that affect even the greatest among us.

Here is where we must make our transition into a study of epistemology as practiced in a biblical theological context. Up to this point, I have set out to give you a taste of your insanity. I have undertaken to bring you face-to-face with the madness that has kept you from truly knowing, or at least from understanding *how* it is, and *why* it is, that you know. What we have seen is that man-made philosophies—the further removed they are from God—produce mixed results at best, and more often than not lead to skepticism. But I must develop theism as an alternative to this purely human thinking. I have yet to demonstrate how human reason—created, sustained, sanctified by God—can give us what we long for.

In the second section of this book we shall continue our exploration of our own insanity and seek to understand if, and how, a biblical model of epistemology can lavish true knowledge upon us. We must now turn our

---

human beings into existence since they will ultimately experience suffering. For more on this madness see Benatar, *Better Never to Have Been*. Benatar's ethics of procreation stand in complete opposition to the Christian view, which validates life and sees the hope in redemption through Jesus Christ.

attention to the problem of *fideism*, which has traditionally created gaps between human reason and divinely inspired faith. After we have looked at the biblical view of faith and its relationship to reason, we will be in a better position to explore the proposition that God is the true source of justified true beliefs about all reality, both physical and spiritual. This will allow us to then understand how God communicates knowledge to us through both general and special revelation. Only through knowledge of God, I shall argue, can the troubles of our insanity be undone.

Have you seen such men? Their tainted minds are wholly unable to separate fact from fiction, truth from lie, rational proof from skepticism. They fumble about blinded by the power of their own Enlightenment ideas. And the thing that blinds them is not an abundantly glorious and amply beautiful light, but a silent, cold, and callous darkness. We are all prone to ignorance, raving mad in the gloom, unable to grasp the extent of our own madness. Who then will awaken us from our insanity?

PART TWO

ASCENT INTO KNOWLEDGE

6

Accidents of Reason

HAVE YOU SEEN SUCH men in the Bible-black darkness of their intellects, injecting their thoughts with ancient scriptural nonsense until all knowledge and sanity are driven from their minds? Have you seen the Bible-thumping thunderers of doomsday gloom, fuming from their pulpits and damning us all with their godforsaken bombast? "If it was good enough for the apostle Paul and for Timothy, then it's good enough for me," they thunder, as they hold the sacred text above their heads with one hand, and with the other, point an outstretched finger of accusation into the hollow depths of our souls. It is their sacred duty to snuff out the very last flicker of reason with the icy wind of mindless, maddening faith. With warnings of the fire and brimstone to come, they implore us to stop resisting and just believe—to stop trusting reason and just take that step off the ledge of sanity.

We have all either heard it or assumed it ourselves: Belief in God is deadly to reason. It is assumed that to accept Christian theism is to forever bind the knowledge-building faculties of the mind and to march dutifully to the weekly Sunday meeting where Holy Writ mutates into strains of bombast that metastasize in the heads of the mindless faithful. To preach Christian theism is to put the pistol to your head and commit the unthinkable: intellectual suicide. Christianity means faith, and faith means insanity.

But we are already insane. Have we not previously established this? Our minds do not function as they should. We are deceived by our own mental operations. We have searched for a cure in skepticism; we have resigned ourselves to overstated promises of pure reason, but these forgeries

PART TWO: ASCENT INTO KNOWLEDGE

of true knowledge have forsaken us. Skepticism has retracted any chance at attaining knowledge by its blatant abandonment of the possibility of justified truths. Our reliance on unaided human reason only moves us further down the bottomless pit of inquiry, with no end in sight. We have seen that those who are weary of skepticism search for solace by the power of human reason. Likewise, we have seen that those who ruminate on the promises of *reasonism* will be sucked back into the never-ending nagging doubts of skepticism. The shortcomings of faulty philosophical reasoning have left us with little choice but to look to answers that come from outside our feeble minds. Knowledge-selling sophists are not what we need.

But if not to mad philosophers, then to whom shall we look for our source of *justified true belief*? To the lunacy of pastors and priests? What devilry could possibly drive us to the sort of knowledge purported by the Christian theist, whether pastor, priest, or philosopher? Their alternative to skepticism, rationalism, and radical empiricism entails blind unthinking faith . . . or does it? To this, I would say no, and would argue fervently to the contrary. Faith need not be blind or unthinking, but joined to our God-given reason. A commitment to blind faith, which rejects the wealth of our philosophical tradition (as flawed as it may be at times), leaves us no better off in our search for the sanity of true knowledge than do all the options examined thus far.

FAITH AND REASON

I dare suggest, and even claim, that faith cannot be rent from reason, though I also realize that this claim may seem unlikely for some and unwelcome for others. For many, the tempestuous relationship between faith and reason may be likened to the equally difficult relationship between a frenzied squirrel and an approaching automobile. Faith is fine as long as it stays within its mystical religious domain as nothing more than a hopeful emotional boost, but if it dares step into the path of dialogue with reason, it will be mercilessly subjugated forthwith.

What a strange concept—faith: the desperate unwillingness to release our worn out mythologies and groundless dreams into the black abyss where they belong. Faith: the belief in what is not, cannot, and must not be true. Faith: the mad preacher's opiate, dispersed like sweet incense to bewitch and beguile reason. It is thought that if faith has anything to do with knowledge, then knowledge might as well be defined as insanity pure and simple.

Or could it be that the so-called dichotomy between faith and reason is little more than an invention of cantankerous atheists who view theists as ignorant magicians bent on mesmerizing the crowds by pulling invisible gods out of hats? This may be, but it is just as likely that theists themselves have invented the dichotomy as a way of keeping their critics at a distance. After all, if faith has nothing to do with reason, then reason can do nothing to harm faith.

With the challenge of this false dichotomy in mind, we must make it our goal to defend a *reasonable* faith against the problem of fideism (which in its most radical form divorces theistic belief from truth and justifiability, making such belief irrational and groundless). And we must demonstrate that God is the Source of all knowledge, not a means by which to escape from knowledge. We must commit ourselves to the idea that faith is a form of religious knowledge that need not be thought of as irrational. Faith most certainly does *not* consist of an unthinking obligation to make-believe. We must understand that every word and promise of God is based on rational, knowable propositions. After all, if it is not *true* and *justifiable* that God exists, that he has given us the capacity to know, and that he speaks to us through Scripture, then any belief we hold concerning him is ludicrously lacking.

What should concern us is a form of fideism that fogs our God-given reason and overreacts to rationality by disposing of it permanently. The very term *fideism* has come to denote suspicion of the rational mind and an overactive enthusiasm for careless leaps and bounds into the shadows. But the label has further been used as a term of abuse, and a straw man to be pulverized by those who do not understand it. Some self-proclaimed fideists pit faith violently against reason, while other philosophers like C. Stephen Evans claim that faith is not against—but rather beyond—reason. The quarrel of the latter is not with reason itself but with intellectual arrogance.

Evans's definition of fideism is helpful as he points out that fideism, which comes from the Latin word for faith, may essentially be replaced by the self-explanatory term "faith-ism."[1] *Faithism*, which places faith at the center of religious knowledge, would logically stand over and against the claims of rationalism, which places human reason at the center. Evans goes on to add that "faith must be accepted as at least partly autonomous or

---

1. Evans, *Faith Beyond Reason*, 8.

independent of reason, or even that reason must in some ways be corrected by or be made subservient to faith."[2] Given this clarification, fideism may be thought of, not as a flight from truth, but as a means by which certain religious truth might be attained. Though Evans's distinctions are helpful, they can easily lead to a separation of Christian faith from all rational discourse. This is the way that nineteenth- century Danish philosopher Søren Kierkegaard approached his faith, saying that no argument from reason could establish the truth of Christianity as could the testimony of faith itself. "Faith is the testimony," said Kierkegaard.[3] "Faith is the justification."[4]

The Kierkegaardian view of faith offers one of the most extreme accounts of fideism in regard to religious knowledge. The idea of faith as a blind leap into the darkness may not have been too far from Kierkegaard's mind. If belief in God is a blind leap into the darkness, then belief in God is not grounded on any true or justified proposition, and if belief in God is not grounded on any true or justified proposition, then it does not constitute knowledge in the traditional sense of the term.

In driving an epistemic wedge between faith and reason, Kierkegaard was protecting Christian belief from the attack of the Enlightenment evidential critiques of religion that had rapidly sprung to life in the two preceding centuries. Moreover, he may have given the faith-based relationship with Christ a more experiential touch by accentuating the mystical, subjective, and existential nature of belief. Kierkegaard did not think that belief in God could or should be established upon evidence independent of faith. If we have reason behind our belief in God's promises, then we do not really have faith, do we? When faith is seen as a belief that steps beyond the world of reason, evidence, and justification, it may seal itself off from reason and all of reason's critiques. For Kierkegaard, that which is beyond and against reason is not prone to reason's harsh attack.

But in separating faith from reason, Kierkegaard also opened the door to the criticism that faith is nothing more than irrational anti-knowledge. This assumption, proliferated by certain Christians, is now a common view of faith among countless people. Harry Blamires laments this digression in contemporary definitions of faith by saying that in recent years . . .

---

2. Ibid., 9. For more on the various forms of fideism and their development in the history of philosophy, see Penelhum, *God and Skepticism*.

3. Søren Kierkegaard, *Provocations*, 270.

4. Ibid., 270.

Accidents of Reason

"Faith" came to be regarded as a kind of provisional presuppositional footing in an as yet unexplored terrain. It was an inferior substitute for knowledge, a substitute that humanity needed only where knowledge was not yet available.[5]

In one of his thoroughly contentious but comical rants against theistic belief, Richard Dawkins claimed that *"faith is one of the world's great evils, comparable to the smallpox virus but harder to eradicate."*[6] The faith of which Dawkins speaks is one that, devoid of evidence, is little more than a vice—"the principle vice of any religion."[7] Dawkins's words echo the cry of Arthur Schopenhauer, whose disdain for faith rang clear in the following words:

> Mankind is growing out of religion as out of its childhood clothes. Faith and knowledge do not get on well together in the same head: they are like a wolf and a sheep in the same cage—and knowledge is the wolf that threatens to eat up its companion.[8]

Spanning the length and breadth of philosophical time and space, the notion that faith and reason are at odds with each other extends beyond the analytical tradition in which Dawkins was bred, and into the continental philosophers of Europe. Counted among these continental thinkers is Luc Ferry, who states that at the core of Christian faith is an "opposition to the rationality at the heart of philosophy."[9] Like his many peers who reject the viability of the Christian God as the best explanation for ultimate reality, Ferry holds that faith supplants reason, requiring that the thoughtful person "hang up" his intelligence, opting instead for blind unthinking devotion.[10] According to Ferry, this inability for the Christian to work things out by "intelligence and reason" is what ultimately deteriorated the Christian institution, allowing it to be razed by a superior Enlightenment philosophy.[11]

The sentiment that faith is in direct and violent opposition to reason has become all-too-common since the Enlightenment dichotomized belief into the scientific reality of knowledge on the one side and the religious

---

5. Blamires, *Post-Christian Mind*, 5.
6. Dawkins, "Science verses Religion," 451.
7. Ibid., 451.
8. Schopenhauer, *Horrors and Absurdities of Religion*, 87–88.
9. Luc Ferry, *Brief History of Thought*, 63.
10. Ibid., 63–65.
11. Ibid., 64.

fantasy of faith on the other. Paul Helm points out the unfortunate reality that "in the eyes of many contemporary philosophers, though by no means most of those that form the mainstream of modern western philosophy from Descartes onwards, no propositions of religion pass, or could ever pass, the test of reason, and so are 'irrational.'"[12] Norman Malcolm echoes this observation:

> In our Western academic philosophy, religious belief is commonly regarded as unreasonable and is viewed with condescension or even contempt. It is said that religion is a refuge for those who because of weakness of intellect or character are unable to confront the stern realities of the world.[13]

This observation likely alludes to the claims of Sigmund Freud that religion is a crutch to help psychologically weak people hobble their way through life. But Malcolm's response to this was not to bring faith and reason together in an attempt to show the validity of religious claims. Rather, he estranged faith and reason all the more. Like Kierkegaard, Malcolm thought that religious belief could not be justified rationally, making it exempt from rational attack.

What has faith to do with reason after all? Kierkegaard believed that rational objective evidence for God serves little purpose. He who has faith in God is already convinced of the truth of Christianity, and he who does not have faith is not going to get it by listening to rational arguments.[14] Faith is a subjective, personal, and passionate relationship to God, not a dry mathematical equation.[15] According to a Kierkegaardian view of knowledge, God exists because I believe he exists, and I can know him because I believe that I do. In a sense, I believe what I believe because I believe it and have experienced it in a realm beyond the nagging voice of reason.

THE BLIND LEAP

Kierkegaard is right to emphasize the importance of a personal relationship with a personal God, as every Christian theist should willingly and gladly attest. At the very center of Christianity shines the cross of Christ that

12. Helm, *Faith and Understanding*, 4.
13. Malcolm, "Groundlessness of Belief," 394.
14. Kierkegaard, "Subjectivity is Truth," 379.
15. Ibid., 379.

allows reconciliation between God and man. Relationship was at the center of God's creative act in making man. Relationship with God was the very thing broken when man fell into sin. Relationship is what Christ came to repair when he gave his life to redeem ours. However, despite Kierkegaard's emphasis on relationship with God, the *insanity* of his radical fideism must be challenged on two fronts.

First, if God can only be *known* through feelings of the heart devoid of rational reflection, then he has nothing to do whatsoever with the tripartite analysis of justified true belief. According to a fideistic paradigm, it would be impossible both for man to possess knowledge of God and for God to serve as a reliable source of knowledge. Our rational assessment of reality would belong to another world entirely. God, while being an object of belief, could hardly be a source of knowledge about any aspect of the universe. We would have nothing by which to evaluate knowledge-claims and would be subsequently led right back into the insanity of skepticism or the madness of seeking a godless rational explanation.

We cannot separate knowledge of physical reality from knowledge of spiritual reality, as if they are two unrelated things. God, a spiritual reality, made the physical universe and interacts with it. The spiritual reality existed before the physical reality. We have wrongly claimed to have knowledge of the world by our rational faculties while viewing God through an irrational faith lens. But if we claim to know the simple objects around us, how much more should we have access to knowledge about the One who made these objects. Likewise, knowing God should open our eyes to the possibility of knowing his world. We have wrongly believed that we can hold justified true beliefs about the world but that this knowledge leads only to blind leaps of faith concerning God. And we have wrongly believed that we must take the Creator's existence on faith while experiencing his creation by knowledge. I would propose, however, that by seeking justified true beliefs about God we will subsequently be led to even greater certainty in our justified true beliefs about the world. There is only one reality—a reality that consists of both the spiritual and the physical. The fullness of this reality can, indeed, be known.

Second, biblical faith requires a rational foundation leading to confidence in the concrete and knowable realities God has revealed. If there is no objectively knowable basis for religious belief, then no religious system of belief could be understood or evaluated from the outside. One would first have to believe in God in order to make any kind of statement, whether true of false, about God. Yet, the possibility of evaluating religious claims seems perfectly plausible. If it were not, no one would be able to think about or assess the truth or falsity of a religious proposition. The irreconcilable differences between two opposing viewpoints could not be open to rational evaluation. With this said, the Christian, more than anyone, should assume that having been created by God, humans possess the capacity to rationally gather and evaluate evidence and arguments. No matter what the fideist says, all beliefs, including irrational leaps into the darkness, are based on some form of evidence.

For example, if you were to ask me if I believe in God, and I were to answer yes, you might then ask me how I know that he is real. If I say it does not matter and that I just have faith that it is so, then I have given at least two pieces of evidence (though not very good ones). First, by sticking to my faith, I have suggested that my cognitive material is functioning well enough for me to unabashedly assert my belief. Second, by giving an object of faith, I have suggested that the existence of God is a believable proposition that can be taken as true. If I were to claim, as many Christians do, that through my faith I have somehow experienced the object of that faith in a real relationship, then I would be adding an experience-based confirmation of God's existence. In other words, while trying to eschew evidence for my faith, I, the fideist, am giving the following evidence: people are capable of holding beliefs, and it is possible to believe that God truly exists. Moreover, I am claiming that by acting in faith, I have encountered God, proving my blind leap to be grounded in a reality that I have personally subjected to an empirical test. Though these are terribly unconvincing arguments for the Christian faith, they are arguments, nonetheless, and are founded on human reason.

Kierkegaard's blind faith undermines the very meaning of biblical faith by accenting a passion of the heart devoid of knowable truth about the real historical Jesus. Passions that remain unguided by knowledge can lead anywhere, not least of all into theological error. The spiritual life must never be reduced to capricious fits of passion no matter how sincere. Passion may bring us closer to God, but to *which* God, exactly, are we being brought closer?

There is no good reason to dedicate yourself to any idea unless you have some evidence for supposing it might be true. This does not mean you must have overwhelmingly conclusive justification for the truth of your faith, but that you must have at least a rational grounding for your faith.

William Clifford famously said that "it is wrong always, everywhere, and for anyone, to believe anything on insufficient evidence."[16] We need not take matters quite this far, since by Clifford's standard, we may never attain perfectly sufficient evidence. Nevertheless, beliefs removed from evidence will likely find themselves hovering over the void. Faith does not and cannot exist when removed from its intellectual and evidential base, but is deepened and clarified by its relationship to God-given reason.[17] The Bible never asks you to jump until it has given evidence for the reliability of the One waiting to catch you when you do, and until it has explained why a jump is necessary in the first place.

TRUE FAITH

Some may object, saying the Bible is filled to overflowing with examples of blind leaps. One might point to the passage that describes faith as "being sure of what we hope for and certain of what we do not see" (Heb. 11:1). But does this suggest a blind leap? Not if we submit ourselves to a more careful reading of the way faith is portrayed in Scripture. The things we hope for but do not see are the promises of things to come made by the God, who has already proven himself faithful in the past.

Consider the example of Abraham in the eleventh chapter of the epistle to the Hebrews. Abraham and his wife, Sarah, were old and as good as dead when God promised them that they would have a child. And though they had reason to be skeptical, we are told that Abraham responded in faith to what God promised would come to pass. Now we might ask whether Abraham was unreasonable or unjustified in his belief that God would give his barren, aged wife a child. But we must also remember that Abraham's faith was not a blind leap. God had already given Abraham evidence to believe. God had spoken to Abraham and had already fulfilled past promises. God had given him reason to believe that his faith was based on a solid foundation.

Suppose that Abraham, having never heard the voice of God, having never received a single promise from God, and having embarked on a spiritual journey filled with one adversity after another, suddenly decided to believe that God would give his post-menopausal wife a child. If this were so, Abraham would be completely unjustified in his belief. He would

---

16. Clifford, *Ethics of Belief*, 77.
17. Helm, *Faith and Understanding*, 15.

be taking a blind and foolish leap into the darkness. But this is far from what the Bible tells us he did. God revealed himself to Abraham, spoke to him, made promises to him, and kept his promises. For Abraham, faith was to simply trust in the One who was logically and reasonably trustworthy.

Another oft misunderstood example of faith in Scripture is seen in the account of the apostle Thomas, in John's gospel chapter 20. Thomas, the dubious doubter, disposed of the idea that Jesus had been resurrected from the dead until he saw the evidence with his own eyes. This example is cited by some fideists to purport blind unthinking faith in Jesus, since Jesus himself states, "Blessed are those who have not seen and yet have believed" (John 20:29). But Jesus is not asking his disciples to heave themselves into a chasm for no apparent reason. He is, rather, challenging the tenacious incredulity of those who have already witnessed hundreds of miracles and have watched as Jesus fulfills one Old Testament prophecy after another, and yet still demand more evidence. If Jesus had not been concerned with evidence, it is doubtful he would have appeared to anyone in his post-resurrection state. Thomas was not wrong to unite his faith to reason; he was wrong to ask for more evidence when plenty had already been given. At some point along the way, God wants our wholehearted trust.

Like Thomas, the Pharisees of Jesus' day made the same recalcitrant request in Matthew's gospel, chapter 12, by asking for a sign of proof that Jesus was their Messiah. "Show us but one simple sign," they said, "and we will trust you, putting our faith in you as our Lord and king." All they wanted was a sign. What could possibly be wrong with that? Why was Jesus so quick to condemn their inquiry as wicked and disobedient when they had merely brought him a humble request? The answer lies in the preceding eleven chapters of Matthew's gospel. Jesus rejected their demands because these were the same Pharisees who had already watched Jesus heal the sick, raise the dead, and calm a storm. He had given them a sign. He had given them many signs. First-century Galilee was a small geographical region where word quickly spread, and it would have been impossible for those living there to ignore what Jesus had already done. Jesus had given them their fair share of evidence and would give them even more. The evidence was already there. What Jesus wanted now was their trust. In the same way, he wants all people everywhere to believe that he will do what he says he will do and be who he says he is: the Son of God.

Others will object, however, that it is God who ultimately gives us the faith to believe him, making any evidence superfluous. A biblical response to this must be yes and no. We should agree that God is our source of saving faith. Anyone who is dead in his sins will lack both the desire and the capacity to raise himself to life (Eph. 2:1–2). Saving faith must originate in the actions of God. But we must also understand that the faith God gives us is not given in spite of the evidence, but in spite of sin. It is not a lack of evidence that restricts us from knowing God, but a problem of sin that blinds and contorts the truth in the face of evidence. The faith God graciously allows us comes by means of the evidences he has placed before us. One such piece of evidence is the gift of faith itself. The fact that we can possess faith while living in a sinful world, where faith should be impossible, is *evidence* in and of itself for the work of God in bringing us to knowledge. The grace of God orients our reasoning toward him and removes the hazy film that covers our eyes. In this way, God can and should be *known* concretely as one who exists in reality and gives us knowledge about reality.

Biblical faith is not a wrong turn on the road of reason. It is not a collision with stupidity. We can have justified true beliefs about spiritual realities because God himself reveals justified truths that can be believed. He shows us that to have faith is to trust in his promises based on the evidence he has revealed. In their first volume of *Integrative Theology*, Gordon Lewis and Bruce Demarest point out that "although the object of faith may be unseen, the evidence for [a] belief is seen and needs to be examined with sound methodology."[18] The labor of reason must take place if faith is to be built. J.P. Moreland emphasizes this point, defining biblical faith as "a power or skill to act in accordance with the nature of the kingdom of God, a trust in what we have reason to believe."[19] Faith is belief in the promises of God, spoken in truth, supported by evidence, and accepted by the reasonable mind. As John Stott puts it, "Faith is a reasoning trust, a trust which reckons thoughtfully and confidently on the trustworthiness of God."[20] For Stott, faith is impossible without thinking.[21] He states that "true faith is essentially reasonable because it trusts in the character and the promises of God."[22] But this *reasonable* faith has been lost on many modern churchgoers and ignored by religious skeptics who prefer to mock a caricature of faith instead.

18. Demarest and Lewis, *Integrative Theology*, 39.
19. Moreland, *Love Your God*, 19.
20. Stott, *Your Mind Matters*, 52.
21. Ibid., 53.
22. Ibid., 49.

PART TWO: ASCENT INTO KNOWLEDGE

The *new* stereotypical blind faith is the faith that has been hijacked by popular psychology and contorted into positive thinking. This reduces faith to little more than wishful thinking. It has become all too common for the faithful to see faith as a wish. If I believe it with all my might, then it will happen. Name your wish, trust that it can be yours, and *voila*, it will come to pass. It is thought that the only thing that can possibly limit your achievement is your own self-defeating doubt. And so you must find a way to make yourself believe. Boil and mix your esoteric religious brew—a bit of Bible dust, a touch of liquid theistic optimism, all your festering hopes and dreams churned and curdled in the black pot. Drink your mind-numbing poison.

If this is all there is to faith, then Christianity has fallen frighteningly far. This point is confirmed when antagonists to Christianity define our faith for us, calling it nothing more than gullibility—a belief in what common sense tells us cannot be true. In this view, faith is taken as something uncritical, undiscerning, and completely unreasonable.[23] This is the faith that religious skeptics like to see. Many would be thrilled to see Christianity confined to a realm of fideistic irrationality.

The imaginary battle between faith and reason, between theology and science, is a ploy to distract us from proper knowledge acquisition. Matters of faith are rarely, if ever, in conflict with matters of reason. This conflict model is at odds with both the biblical mandate to rule over the earth and create civilization through knowledge (Gen. 1:27–31; Ps. 8), and the historical evidence which suggests men of faith were the true founders of modern science.[24] Likewise, any model of faith and reason that calls for complete divergence between the two reduces knowledge to that which can only be explained within a materialist framework. This moves questions of God and morality to a realm of speculation. By this divorce, knowledge of both physical and spiritual realities is weakened.[25] Faith, then, is left to the madman.

Fortunately, however, faith is not an empty wish or fool's credulity but an intellectually satisfying confidence in propositions that have been bathed in truth and justification. Fideism, as a rejection of reason and as an

---

23. Ibid., 49.

24. Further details on the Christian influence on modern science can be found in chapter 7.

25. For a good summary of *Conflict Model*, the *Independence Model*, and the *Convergence Model* of theology and science, see DeWeese, "Theology and Science," 36–39. See also DeWeese, *Doing Philosophy*.

antithesis to knowledge, is not an intellectually satisfying alternative to the extremes of skepticism or rationalism. It makes, rather, for little more than another form of insanity.

When faced with philosophically difficult questions in Scripture, far too many Christians forego intellectual rigor in favor of theological contradiction. But according to theologian R. C. Sproul, logical contradictions have no place in careful Christian reflection. Sproul notes this:

> I hear statements like, "God is bigger than logic!" or "Faith is higher than reason!" to defend the use of contradiction in theology. I certainly agree that God is bigger than logic and that faith is higher than reason. I agree with all my heart and with all my head. What I want to avoid is a God who is smaller than logic and a faith that is lower than reason. A God who is smaller than logic would be and should be destroyed by logic. A faith that is lower than reason is irrational and absurd.[26]

Reason assures the safety of our next step but will not take that step itself. Faith is higher than reason in that it dares to tread where reason will not go. Biblical faith takes seriously the promises of God in history and acts on them. In matters of trust, fideism rightly demands the courage to believe—courage that is absent from skepticism. Furthermore, it does not shy away from seemingly foolhardy optimism—optimism that is absent from rationalism and radical empiricism. What renders fideism absurd is that it wrongly creates an anti-rational mindlessness that weakens religious knowledge and filters down to hinder our knowledge of the physical universe.

The dearth of both evidential and scriptural support for fideism is reason enough to reject it. Woe betide us if we embrace this leap into the darkness and fall, with the skeptic and the rationalist, into the pit of nitwits. Fideism, in its pious embrace of rationally ungrounded trust, succumbs to the same shortcomings as skepticism and rationalism by basing knowledge in man. This may seem like an overzealous attempt to bury all of man's intellectual shortcomings in the same overcrowded grave, but, on the other hand, fideism makes man the center of the leap. It makes his knowledge of God a condition of his own daredevil volitional fortitude. We have already seen that in the search for sanity, skepticism leads to the despairing realization that knowledge is not possible. Likewise we have seen that the exploits of rationalism and radical empiricism lead to empty pride in a knowledge

---

26. Sproul, *Chosen by God*, 40.

PART TWO: ASCENT INTO KNOWLEDGE

that is not attainable. Fideism embraces the worst of both worlds. Like skepticism, blind faith leads to the despairing awareness that justified true beliefs are beyond us. Like rationalism, it places our sovereign judgment at the center of what is known. Fideism centers not on what God gives us through how he reveals himself in nature, in Scripture, and in Christ Jesus, but on what we give him through our courageous willingness to believe before we even have a first impression. Fideism asks us if we are man enough to jump. It is a dare and a wager against all odds.

The dangerous dichotomy created by fideism breaks man in two. On the one hand, we have a man intellectually frozen by irrationality as he contemplates spiritual beliefs. On the other hand, we have a man forced to look to the insanity of skepticism and rationalism as a foundation for his beliefs about the world. Instead of explaining our knowledge of both religious and nonreligious truths, fideism leaves us confused as never before.

Faith is not a fool's game of chance or an imaginary rope tied to our feet as we plummet blissfully to our death. It is not a ninny's hope that the flying spaghetti monster will one day return and take us away to live in the land of Parmesan and Oregano beyond the Meatball Mountains where our cares will forever be forgotten. Faith is more certain than a role of the dice or a wager on mere possibilities even when the evidence is not in our favor. Faith is not the mind of an ignorant child in the body of a man. It is neither a medical condition from which we need to be cured nor a ticket into an elitist religious club. True faith would hardly recognize such nonsense and would likely laugh at such absurdities. Faith is an utter confidence in the promises of a fully trustworthy God who is the Source and Giver of knowledge and the only guarantee that we can truly know anything. While fideism attempts to point us to God, it only succeeds at estranging us from knowledge. What we really need is to be brought closer to the God who serves as our only hope for knowledge. The madman has no other assurance.

As the red sun of dusk settles behind the hills, you will see him running out of the woods, a mere shadow in the twilight, his unkempt hair flailing against his naked body as he hoots and whistles his way across the pasture lands, laughing and squealing with delight as he chases rabbits and squirrels. In a flying somersault, he will snatch the moon from the sky, giggle, and eat it in several large bites. Then he will lie in the grass, clutching his stomach and moaning with indigestion. In his crazed eyes, you can see that he believes what he believes because he wants to believe it. Keep watching. In only a moment's time, the crepuscular lunatic will pick himself up and without a care in the world dance and pirouette his way into the sunset. He is a madman after all. Without a proper understanding of what he knows and the extent to which he knows it, his mind is not quite right. He is *funny* in the head. He is a radical fideist.

7

God Thinks, Therefore, I Am

THE VULTURE GLIDED GRACEFULLY through the cloudless sky, circling, now descending upon him to peck out his liver as it had done the day before. Forever chained to the side of the mountain, Prometheus had eternity to contemplate his act of defiance against the chief of the gods. He had brought man the knowledge of fire and incited the wrath of Mount Olympus. Human knowledge could not be tolerated and the successes brought on by man's knowledge were a threat against heaven itself. Zeus, chief of the gods, in his caprice, was easily offended by the achievements of the Greeks, whose most formidable struggle lay not in economic and political uncertainty but in anticipating what might provoke the gods to abandon their revelry and hurl their hexes and calamity on the offenders below. Man had no greater enemy than a god inflamed with envy. But even the caprice of the gods would not hinder the early philosophers from going about their work of asking *why*.

Today, the gods of old have passed away, having died of too much drink, too much sex, and too much human disbelief in their existence. Their homes are abandoned as the Acropolis in Athens continues to crumble on its perch, exposed to the uncaring elements. They have been forsaken even by the philosophers, whose diaspora has led their kind to seek an audience in other distant lecture halls throughout the world. The ancient white stones sit in silence, not to be disturbed by the echoing debates of men, the memories of whom have largely faded from our daily thoughts and lives.

God Thinks, Therefore, I Am

But this is hardly surprising. The cadaverous remains of human progress will be found wherever we establish ourselves, reminding us of our glorious past and our clouded future. The philosopher's dialectics never cease, and the questions once posed remain with the same daunting force, driving us to reflection and debate and contributing all the more to our epistemic bewilderment. The feeble phantoms of Mount Olympus cannot silence our thirst for knowledge. And so we rave, we rage, and we rant in debate for the hope and the comfort of a justified true belief.

Have you seen such men? Of course you have, for you are one of them. You belong to the race of those whose feeble efforts at attaining knowledge have failed. You have breathed the same air, walked the same earth, and sacrificed to the same gods as the whole of humanity. You have participated in all its futile efforts at knowing. Like Eve, you have forsaken true knowledge by lusting after a lie. Like Pyrrho, you have flirted with the black void of doubt never to overcome it. Like Luther, you have boldly posted your intellectual reservations on dogma's door in an act of defiance. You rail against the jumbled creeds that stifle the truth as it lies obscured beneath layers of popish vestment. Like Plato and Descartes, you have thirsted for reason's assuring comfort only to open a bottomless pit of questions. Like the apostle Thomas, you long to justify your beliefs with indubitable justification. Like Kierkegaard, you have passionately thrown yourself into the chasm of faith in search of a sure foundation. And like all of them, you are insane.

I will say no more to convince you of your insanity because no more needs to be said. Now is the moment for us to make our escape. We have seen our condition of ignorance and the futility of our efforts at truly knowing. We have seen that the only knowledge available to our confused minds is the knowledge of our own cognitive confusion. But that gets us nowhere. So let us turn and flee the darkness of skepticism and its cohorts. The escape of which I speak is much more than a desperate bolt toward a pinpoint of light in a black abyss. It is, rather, a step into a full and glorious illumination. I have alluded to it before and so it will hardly surprise you.

Here is our escape. Our one fixed point, our source of knowing, our certainty, and our foundation for knowledge is simply this: God, the all-knowing infinite Knower, Creator and Sustainer of human justified true beliefs. God is the only viable possibility for establishing human knowledge. The philosophers cannot do it, nor can the deities of our own making muster the strength to guarantee our beliefs. The madmen of the world must resign themselves to this simple answer.

For some, however, it will seem much too simple and far too convenient. "God, a source of knowledge? Ha! A source of stupidity perhaps." "When all other explanations fail," they laugh, "just make up a story about God." "When the intellectual challenge gets tough," they sneer, "the tough fill in knowledge gaps with invisible beings who offer easy solutions to all our dilemmas." To them, God is nothing more than a god of the gaps. Why, given enough time and research, God will not be needed to explain difficulties that science will ultimately dismantle. The divine gap-filler will be replaced with real knowledge, or so it is thought. But as we have seen, real knowledge can never be achieved so long as we live in a godless universe. It is naïvely assumed that the next three-thousand years of philosophy will untangle the problems created by the last three-thousand years of philosophy. Just give it some more time.

But time is not the issue. We have devoted plenty of time to answering epistemology's biggest questions, but without God, the more time we give it the further we move from the answer. We have already seen that the radical empiricism that sprang from the Enlightenment can do nothing to reconcile knowledge with materialism. Skepticism is the best we will ever obtain on our own. The mere possibility of knowing anything depends absolutely on God. There is no other way. This is not an ungrounded and fatuous locution, pulled from a hat so that our knowledge gaps might be temporarily filled. Our foundation for knowledge must be God.

When Descartes' plume left the words *cogito ergo sum* scratched on a piece of paper all those years ago, he did much for the world of philosophy thereafter, but erred greatly in one thing. It is not the individual's thought that guarantees our being, as he had presumed.[1] Descartes' *cogito* had been turned inward when it should have been turned outward. Not our thought, but God's thought, guarantees our existence and our knowledge of that existence. *God thinks, therefore, I am.* His thought serves as the creative force behind human existence. In this way, his very thoughts generated the creation of the world, the creation of man, and the creation of man's cognitive capacities. Without a divine and infinite mind to guide and guarantee the knowledge of finite beings, we cannot hope to overcome the deficiencies imposed by our cognitive malfunction, by our . . . insanity.

---

1. As noted in chapter 4, Descartes employs an argument from mind to prove God's existence and solidify man's source of knowledge. God is not, however, his starting point.

God Thinks, Therefore, I Am

There is great irony in denying God as the ultimate Source of knowledge, for to claim knowledge that God does not exist, or that he is unknowable, is to assume his existence in the first place. Since God is the only viable explanation for knowledge, any argument brought against him must presuppose his existence. The folly of claiming to possess justified true beliefs while denying the existence of God may be likened to the folly of claiming to be a mother while denying the existence of children, or claiming to be a dentist while denying the existence of teeth.

The previous chapters have led us to the conclusion that *God is the Source and Guarantee of all knowledge and the means by which insanity is to be overcome.* And I mean with all intentionality to overstate this point because it is of utmost importance. Only the everlasting God can loosen the straitjacket, clear the foggy mind, and guide the madman into the light of day. Only God can *warrant* our understanding and guide us to the knowledge of him in which we will find salvation from our fallen state.

GOOD AND BAD DOGMA

On this matter, three simple points must be made. The first is that *the necessity of God's existence in guaranteeing knowledge-claims is not a conclusion that is arrived at by latching onto naïve and unthinking dogmatism.* We live in an age where the tenuous accusation of dogmatism is hastily bolstered against anyone who dares to claim a definite or final answer to any problem—scientific, philosophical, historical, or the like. An American philosopher, Roderick Chisholm, made this clear when he stated this:

> We all are acquainted with people who think they know a lot more than in fact they do know. I'm thinking of fanatics, bigots, mystics, various types of dogmatists.[2]

He adds these thoughts:

> And as we know, people tend to become dogmatists, temporarily, as a result of the effects of alcohol, or drugs, or religious and emotional experiences. Then they claim to have an inside view of the world and they think they have a deep kind of knowledge giving them a key to the entire workings of the universe.[3]

---

2. Chisholm, "Problem of the Criterion," 9.
3. Ibid., 9.

Chisholm makes it clear that those with a healthy common sense will find some discomfort with such an extreme.[4]

Chisholm's claims are not wholly unfounded. As much as we respect those who have attained a great deal of knowledge, we humans often hold suspect anyone who claims anything with certainty.[5] The more certain you claim to be, the more likely you are to be labeled pejoratively as a dogmatist. This is altogether unpleasant, especially if you are a Christian, since participation in the Christian religion requires assent to numerous dogmatic tenets based in Scripture (the final authority on questions of Christian doctrine). The accusation of dogmatism is even more unpleasant if you are a Christian philosopher since, as "everyone" knows, Christian philosophers have never been able to achieve the liberating, free-spirited satisfaction in life and in knowledge enjoyed by their atheistic counterparts. Descartes, a Catholic, was a dogmatist. Hume, a religious skeptic, was a free-thinker. Pascal, a devout Christian, must have been an idiot. Nietzsche, an atheist, was a liberator of minds. Jonathan Edwards, a Protestant minister and scholar, could only have been a fool.

And we could easily go on because as "everyone" also knows, a Christian explanation of knowledge must be a dogmatic mess. Dogma is bad. Skepticism is good. Dogma comes from Christians. Christians are bad. Atheists are good because dogma is bad and atheists are skeptical and rational, which is good. But dogma is good when good atheists are dogmatic about good things like atheism, which is good. So dogma is good and Christians are bad, especially when they try to develop new ideas in philosophy and reject atheistic dogmas, which are also good. Christians are only good when they let atheists do the thinking, which isn't such a bad thing. Or is it?

We did not arrive at the conclusion that God is the Source and Guarantee of all knowledge simply because it seemed like a good idea after drinking too much Communion wine one Sunday morning. Theism is offered as the only reasonable alternative to the ludicrous intellectual springe imposed by skepticism and the irrational certainty proposed by the ironically uncertain radical empiricist. The skeptic is an antagonist to knowledge, who flees in its wake. The devotee to human reason is not a free-thinker but an unthinking automaton who has been preprogrammed by his equally unthinking

---

4. Ibid., 10.

5. This is true even of certain postmodern Christian thinkers who end up promoting a kind of inescapable relativism when dealing with hermeneutics of any kind.

mother, Madam Cosmos, a non-sentient woman who is yet to achieve any knowledge of her own. With this said, there is more than ample reason to eschew both of these epistemic traps.

Dogma, which is espoused by belief with a good deal of confidence, is not necessarily a bad thing. It is only a problem when we are dogmatic about the wrong things and try to back our claims with insubstantial evidence. Claims of dogmatic proportions are made every day about all sorts of things to which objections are rarely raised. Surprisingly, dogmatism hardly seems to be a problem for most people when applied to simple claims about our world. We are dogmatic about the idea that cows produce milk, and as we add a touch of cream to our tea or coffee, no one could convince us otherwise. When we rise from our beds each morning, we are dogmatic about the idea that sufficient sleep is necessary for good health. We are dogmatic about the idea that we live on a planet, that fish live in the sea, and that Sweden is a country. We are dogmatic about our perceived physical states. If I feel ill, I can announce this sentiment with dogmatic fervor and no one would likely object. We bloviate dogmatically about such things with surprising frequency and no one else seems to care. But when theism is proposed as the best explanation for justified true beliefs, many of us begin to grow rather nervous. Likewise, absolute statements about ethical principles are treated with the same intellectual discomfort. These, we are told, are preferences that ought never to be taken as absolutes.

The point is simply this: If dogmatism is taken as confidence in a certain belief or set of beliefs, then we are all dogmatists, including Chisholm, who dogmatically condemned dogmatism. Whether we like it or not, the word *dogmatist* is a pejorative term, and there is little the theist can do to escape being labeled as one. But given the choice between skeptical dogmatism, rationalistic dogmatism, and theistic dogmatism, we are best off taking our stand with the theist whose "dogma" finally offers us a full-orbed account of both the source and use of real knowledge. If the accusation of dogmatism is nothing more than a last-ditch effort against theists by those who have worked out a purely scientific explanation of their position, then the theist need not be concerned. The theist's dogma carries more epistemic weight and reliance on good sense than that of the skeptic, rationalist, and radical empiricist combined.

PART TWO: ASCENT INTO KNOWLEDGE

THE UNIVERSE CAN BE KNOWN

This brings us to the second point concerning God as the Source and Guarantee of all knowledge: *His existence opens up the possibility of possessing knowledge about the physical universe.* Since there is a God, we can have knowledge about the world. The rational faculties we share with our Creator naturally nudge us toward our surroundings, imploring us to explore that which has been ordered and sustained by him. Even the limits imposed by our finite intelligence do not restrict us from understanding certain intricacies of our world or certain workings of the universe. We can, at very least, approach the universe as something knowable.

Sadly, however, the affirmation of theism as a basis for scientific inquiry has fallen out of favor in a scientific community monopolized by materialistic assumptions. In keeping with modern intellectual fashion, many have wrongly assumed that the practice of natural philosophy is acceptable only if the practitioner holds unswervingly to certain anti-theistic presuppositions. *Oh, how times have changed.* In the past, scientific inquiry was performed largely, if not exclusively, in a theistic context by scholars who were looking to understand God's creation. It was assumed that if God truly made everything in the world, including our rational faculties, then our susceptibility to the constant threat of skepticism would, by consequence, be eradicated. In essence, hypotheses can only be tested and conclusions drawn in a world governed by a creator. The possibility of scientific knowledge depends on God as the Source of knowledge, for as we have seen, the modern radical empiricism assumed by many scientists is antagonistic to science, failing to account for proper function and insufficiently justifying the idea that the world it observes is the world that really exists. It borrows the concept of a knowable universe from theism, while throwing God into the garbage bin. In a way, the radical empiricist munches on rinds, pits, and husks while pitching every part that hints at nutrition or edibility. Lacking God, the atheist has made his universe into a skeletal mess of pieces that cannot be joined into a coherent explanatory system. And though the skeletal structure is necessary, skeletons themselves remain distasteful objects that require a proper and complex covering if they are to form a complete man.

Theism provides this completion and was, at one time, the engine that drove modern science. History abounds with examples of scientists working from the motivation that the existence of God gives way to a knowable world. For the Christian, heavenly bodies were not deities to be revered, but

God Thinks, Therefore, I Am

created objects to be examined. Nature was not something to be feared, but something to be discovered.

Before there was Richard Dawkins, there were Leonardo da Vinci and Andreas Vesalius, Christian theists whose study of human physiology was ground-breaking. Before there was Carl Sagan, there were Nicolaus Copernicus, Johannes Kepler, and Galileo Galilei, also Christian theists whose revolutionary work in astronomy opened our eyes to the vastness of the universe.[6] Before there was Stephen Hawking, there were Isaac Newton and Blaise Pascal, followers of Christ whose discoveries in physics and mathematics are still looked on in admiration as they guide us even today.[7]

Some are convinced that Christianity has done nothing for science and that the brilliant theists of our world are no more than renegades against their own principles, whose knowledge is at odds with their religion. Arthur Schopenhauer summarizes this conviction with a biting claim, saying that "throughout the entire Christian era theism has lain like an incubus on the intellectual, especially philosophical endeavor, and has prevented or stunted all progress."[8] We might agree with Schopenhauer that there are times and places where this may have been true. But the sweeping accusation he gives is much more an invention of anti-religious post-Enlightenment *scientism* than a conclusion of fair and vigorous study in the history of ideas.

Schopenhauer's statement contains nothing close to the truth of the matter, but even so, it is useless to argue over who is more intelligent, Christians or atheists, or to squabble over who has done more for philosophy, theists or skeptics. Insanity affects us all. My point here is only to show that with God as their Source of knowledge, Christians have more than ample reason to pursue justified true beliefs about the physical universe and equally ample reason to discard the absurdities that have often plagued our world. But this motivation does not necessarily make the Christian more intellectually capable than anyone else. We have all heard of the preacher who, after teaching on the creation of Eve from Adam's rib, declared, "That, my friends, is why, to this very day, men have one less rib than women."

---

6. Modern science texts often paint these men as victims of the Church's cruelty and intolerance toward scientists and philosophers. However, like today, the persecution and censorship was fueled more by politics and rivalries than by biblically-based opposition.

7. For more on Christianity's influence on science, the arts, and the development of the West, see Schmidt, *How Christianity Changed the World*. See also Stark, *Victory of Reason*.

8. Schopenhauer, *Horrors and Absurdities of Religion*, 8.

PART TWO: ASCENT INTO KNOWLEDGE

Had he simply verified, he would have saved himself a considerable amount of embarrassment. But ignorance about the world was never an exclusively Christian problem. Aristotle, for example, believed that women possessed fewer teeth than men, a misjudgment he could easily have remedied had he simply taken the time to count. Similarly, Julius Caesar, having trusted the testimony of the locals instead of looking with his own eyes, had this to say about the animals that lived in the forests on the Roman frontiers:

> There are also [animals] which are called elks. The shape of these, and the varied color of their skins, is much like roes, but in size they surpass them a little and are destitute of horns, and have legs without joints and ligatures; nor do they lie down for the purpose of rest, nor, if they have been thrown down by any accident, can they raise or lift themselves up. Trees serve as beds to them; they lean themselves against them, and thus reclining only slightly, they take their rest; when the huntsmen have discovered from the footsteps of these animals whither they are accustomed to betake themselves, they either undermine all the trees at the roots, or cut into them so far that the upper part of the trees may appear to be left standing. When they have leant upon them, according to their habit, they knock down by their weight the unsupported trees, and fall down themselves along with them.[9]

Anyone who has observed an elk could easily contest Caesar's botched zoology, which goes to show that though knowledge of the world is possible, the acquisition of it is not free of the numerous hazards that plague it. Laziness, human error, and lack of sufficient brain power lead us to make more than our fair share of scientific gaffes.

On the other hand, scientific knowledge has exploded in the last century alone. Our ingenuity has led us to solve enigmas, to peer into the depths of space, to understand the infinitesimal particles that surround us, and to build machines that have carried us to the heavens. It seems there is no end to the discoveries we will make. All this ingenuity is possible because we can have scientific knowledge, and all this scientific knowledge is possible because there is a God. In essence, humans can have knowledge about the physical world, not because they are Christian theists but because God exists. Each of us can approach the universe with common sense realism. We can step out our front door and trust that the pavement will support us because we can verify the solidity of the earth and force of gravity.

---

9. Julius Caesar, *Gallic Wars*, Book 6, 27.

God Thinks, Therefore, I Am

Ultimately, we can trust these measurements and the pieces of knowledge they produce because there is a source of knowledge: God. On this second point I beseech you to retain, if nothing else, this: The existence of God is, in and of itself, our justification for knowledge about the physical world.

GOD CAN BE KNOWN

Treatments for mental illness have varied greatly over the centuries, contingent to some extent on the ethical leanings of the medical practitioner. There was an era when mental patients, subjected to the nefarious nature of their doctors, were chained naked to beds or walls, cuffed with iron bars that prohibited movement, or simply confined to cages.[10] Unable to move more than a few feet in any direction, the insane were tortured until either the life or the madness was driven out of them. They were extracted from society and imprisoned so the contagions that were thought to make them fools would not be spread to others. Asylum cells were so inhumanly bad that they were said to be "redolent of shit, straw, and stench," and the beastlike creatures that dwelt there were less esteemed than cattle.[11] It was once believed that the good sense must literally be beaten back into the mental patient, and so it was—mercilessly. Only a wrecked body could heal a wrecked mind.

But to treat the fallen intellectual condition, the pervasive irrationality, and the distortion of cognitive faculties that we have called *insanity* requires a transformation of the mind that is beyond the reach of any cure we alone can administer. To lock ourselves away in dungeons until our irrationality withers with the flesh on our bones is hardly a reasonable solution. Nor can the flagellation of our now cadaverous bodies bring our minds back to life. If we are to be rid of our insanity and come to our senses, it will not be by regular purges, vomits, or bleedings. Swallowing bubbling tonics and changing our dietary regime will do little to make us sane. The insanity—the knowledge problem—that affects us is far too unrelenting in its subjugation of our cognitive faculties. To be human is to suffer this condition, and to ignore the God who saves us from it is to worsen our miserable lot.

My third and final point concerning God as the ultimate Source of knowledge is tied to our actual knowledge of God. *Since there is a God,*

10. Scull, *Madness*, 48.
11. Ibid., 48.

PART TWO: ASCENT INTO KNOWLEDGE

humans can know not only the physical world, but the immaterial reality of God himself. As obvious as it may seem, a knowable God is the only kind of God worth knowing. What good is there in the God of the deist who winds up the clockwork of the universe only to promptly step away, leaving us alone to figure it all out for ourselves? If that is all there is to God, we are better off denying his existence all together. If God created us with the capacity to know everything except the Creator, then what was his purpose in creating us? We only waste our time bothering with a God of this sort.

Likewise, the impersonal divine force that occupies everything in the universe, according to the pantheistic religions, fails to bring knowledge of God any closer to humanity than does deism. An impersonal unthinking force of this kind can neither possess knowledge nor foster knowledge in man. Like the distant and aloof God of deism, such a God is not worth knowing. But these impersonal deities are a far cry from the God revealed in Scripture who created us not only so we might gain knowledge of the creation, but also that we might gain knowledge of the Creator.

We are made to know him. The *Westminster Shorter Catechism*, which has served as a foundational Protestant document for centuries, asks, "What is the chief end of man?" The response taught by the catechism and grounded in Scripture is that "Man's chief end is to glorify God, and to enjoy him forever" (Rom. 11:36; Rev. 4:11).[12] God made us to know him, to glorify him, and to enjoy him, and this we must hasten to do. How we ought to go about knowing him is a question that will be answered in more detail in chapters 8 and 9, but for now we must recognize that our knowledge of God comes to us from God (Prov. 2:1–8). It is God's desire that our knowledge of him would bring about a greater end still: relationship with him. The Divine Knower has supplied us with the means by which we can possess knowledge, not only *of him* but also *for him, by him, in him*, and *through him* (Rom. 11:36). God intends that our knowledge of him would lead us to an intimate relationship with him, that he might be cherished and enjoyed for eternity. This was the prayer of the apostle Paul for the church in Ephesus in the first century AD. He urged his brothers and sisters in Christ to deepen their knowledge of God and God's salvific works that this knowledge might, in turn, serve to deepen their relationship with their Lord (Eph. 1:17–21).

---

12. *Westminster Shorter Catechism*, question 1.

God Thinks, Therefore, I Am

God thinks, therefore, I am.[13] God thinks, therefore, I think. God's rational capacities permeate the human mind, allowing us the ability to know both him and the world he made. Though our epistemic shortcomings have made us insane, we have the means by which to overcome our madness if we will only acknowledge our source of knowledge and let that knowledge be guided by God. We, whose knowledge-producing faculties have malfunctioned and left us to skepticism, radical rationalism and empiricism, and all-out denial of God, do not constitute normalcy. All of us are born in the camp of insanity. All of us have lived there. And many of us will stay there for the sheer comforts it offers. Ignorance is bliss, especially ignorance about God. After all, the more we know about God, the more he will expect of us. He may even ask for our wholehearted repentance and commitment to him. This may be more than many of us can bear, leading us, rather, to opt for madness. But insanity is not and cannot be normal. Likewise, cognitive malfunction is not and cannot be normal. Ignorance is not and must not ever be the norm.

Scripture personifies knowledge as a woman whose sentinel guard over wisdom and good counsel protects passers-by from folly (Prov. 8:1–3). She speaks what is true and harkens us to heed her advice. But she is much more than a beautiful mistress to be enjoyed for a time and discarded on a whim. She is the wife of our youth, our covenant bride, to whom we must cling with unfaltering and fervent commitment. She offers us the beauty of her mind and the fullness of her delicate intricacies that wait expectantly to be explored. To honor and keep her is to experience the ever-increasing and ample riches of God's creation. She is a lovely lady indeed, her company desirable, her affection life-altering. There is no sweeter sound than the priceless pronouncements whispered from her lips (Prov. 8:6–7). She is a gift to man from the mind of God, "appointed from eternity, from the beginning, before the world began" (Prov. 8:23). Scripture calls us repeatedly to listen to her voice and to seek her company (Prov. 8:4). She is the object of a discerning heart and the treasure that outshines precious stones (Prov. 15:14; 18:15; 20:15). She leads us, step by step, up from the abyss of madness.

---

13. This statement is only intended to demonstrate the Christian belief that man's existence originated in God's creative intellect. It should not be taken as an affirmation of Bishop George Berkeley's idealist theory of knowledge, which purports that reality consists of nothing more than minds and ideas. For Berkeley, the universe has no physical qualities but exists only as an idea in the mind of God. See Berkeley, *Treatise Concerning the Principles of Human Knowledge*.

PART TWO: ASCENT INTO KNOWLEDGE

Why then do we commit intellectual adultery by discarding wisdom for folly? Why do we opt for stupidity, whose siren call so rudely draws us in, attempting to whore itself to us from the dark shadows of insanity? Why do we loiter at the door of foul hags and mind-nags, subjecting ourselves to the corrosive hexes of harpies? The further we are from God, our Source of knowledge, the more susceptible to madness we become. This is why those redeemed by God's grace, and whose minds are being restored, must resist the barrage of vulgar insanities that divert us from truly knowing (Rom. 12:2).

The resistance to knowledge is quite easy. To do it we must simply continue to subject ourselves to every mind-numbing distraction that comes along. We must simply put roadblocks before our minds so as to arrest any possibility of thinking. We must flip a switch, light a screen, or plug various stereophonic devices into our ears. We must prevent rational reflection by listlessly staring with near Zen-like indifference at inert entertainment devices.[14] We must, in essence, distract ourselves. And this is as easily done as it is said since there is no shortage of diversions available to us, whether we want them or not. If we cannot bear the truth, we need to ensure that seeing it is impossible. The blindfolds of diversion are perfect for this.

Diversion may very well be the most formidable enemy of justified true belief. Man has always found ways to divert himself from thinking about the ultimate questions of life, death, meaning, and salvation. Even in the seventeenth century, Pascal commented on the use of gambling, hunting, and billiards for the distraction of humanity and the avoidance of thoughtful reflection.[15] Pascal would likely turn in his grave were he to see the diversion machines that man has made for himself in present times. Only by throwing off diversion and turning our knowledge-building faculties back toward their Creator, can we hope to know rightly.

If God exists, we can confidently possess knowledge in areas of ethics, mathematics, philosophy, biology, chemistry, geology, anthropology, psychology, geography, astronomy, history, medicine, physics, and the like. And where does all the knowledge of such disciplines lead the madman? This will be the goal of the next two chapters, in which we will examine how God has made himself known to us. There, we will study two forms of knowledge that theologians refer to as *natural revelation* and *special*

---

14. Lack of rational reflection is aptly compared with Zen meditation because the point of such meditation is to empty the mind of all rational thought that inhibits the possibility of enlightenment. For more on Zen meditation and practice, see Suzuki, *What is Zen?*

15. Pascal, *Pensées*, 136/139.

revelation—two means used by God to make himself known to humanity, leading to the culmination of knowledge in relationship with God through Jesus Christ.

Have you seen such men who, with clarity of mind, explore the wisdom of the universe with gratitude for their Creator? Have you seen such men who live their lives free from the nagging doubts of skepticism, because they know that God is their Source of knowledge? They have accepted the limits of the human mind and abandoned the despair of rationalism and radical empiricism, opting rather for a fixed point that ensures their knowledge of the world and is found only in God. Have you seen such men who dwell comfortably in the light of day and who view the world through the lens of realism and common sense? They do not doubt the world. They do not fear the world. They are not bound to speculations about a blind, cold, godless universe. Clarity lights their path and knowledge is their aim. Wisdom hides them in her wings and shines her light upon them. Have you seen such men? The Divine Source of all knowledge is their unshakable foundation, opening before them a world where justified true belief is possible.

8

Opening the Book of Nature

BENEATH THE TOWERING GOTHIC edifice and through the murky haze of its vaulted bowels, the sunlight—filtered and sanitized by colored glass—rests delicately upon a piece of ancient machinery, the likes of which are now little more than an oddity of an ostentatious past. A thousand gears and parts grind and groan in unison as the astronomical clock of the Strasbourg Cathedral measures, with a display of elegance and beauty, the relative positions of the sun, moon, and zodiacal constellations. With impeccable precision, small figures step out of their chambers to announce the passing of each hour, their movements accompanied by the punctuating cry of an automated rooster. Adorned with angels, this antique apparatus hails the movements of a clockwork universe. Its creators were no less than the most ingenious of artists. Only the greatest clockmakers and the brightest architects of automatons could have crafted this masterpiece whose constant clicking complexity still attests to their greatness.

    Gaze at a work of this magnitude and you will see a creator at its origin. Magnificence always has a story to tell, and one of the finest is told, not by the clockwork of a clock, but by the clockwork of the universe—colossal in magnitude, overwhelming in beauty, and lavished in mysteries waiting to be discovered. Through an unfathomable expanse of space, we can observe the violence of a dying star as it explodes and spews its entrails into the heavens. Elsewhere, balls of rock and gas are hurled through the void as they orbit their stars. You would never know it by simply looking up into the night sky. Galactic catastrophes of every kind have taken place billions

Opening the Book of Nature

of light-years away in a cold black expanse whose vastness alone is frightening to contemplate.

In gazing at the clockwork of nature we might just see a Creator at its origin. At least, this has been the claim of theologians and God-fearing scientists throughout the centuries. Traditionally, *natural theology* (the study of the ways in which God reveals his existence and character in nature) has purported that the clicking and ticking of the tick-tock universe attest to the existence of a wise and grand Designer, whose infinite knowledge defies the insanity of a world whose cognitive dyslexia prohibits it from reading the sign inscribed "answer" that points beyond itself.[1]

Questions about this sign and where it points emerge naturally from the discipline of natural theology and scientific inquiry. Within this semiotic framework, the universe is an indicator. The sign has to point somewhere. Exactly what this *somewhere* is, however, constitutes the central concern of *natural theology*, which asserts that knowledge of God is inferred through his *general revelation*: the means by which he makes himself known in nature.

Having concluded that the existence of God (the Creator, a Supreme Being) is the only epistemic conclusion that allows us refuge from insanity and confidence in both our cognitive capacities and possession of justified true belief, we are now able to engage in the study of God's general revelation with the aid of natural theology, which is itself a framework for understanding the natural world. Two approaches can be taken to natural theology, each of which is complementary to the other, allowing for greater knowledge of both God and the world. One approach views nature as the sign pointing to God. The other views God as the means by which we might understand nature. And while each of these makes a significant contribution to our knowledge of both the natural world and God, neither will be sufficient in attaining the *personal* justified true beliefs about God that lead to ultimate salvation from insanity.

---

1. William Paley, in his book *Natural Theology*, which was first published in 1802, uses the analogy of clockwork to describe the universe and the designer behind it. Paley's argument is an early example of the work done in inferring the existence of God from the beauty and order of nature.

PART TWO: ASCENT INTO KNOWLEDGE

A SIGN POINTING TO GOD

For centuries, natural theology has viewed the universe as an indicator, flashing evidence of God's existence. However, this sign is not quite as obvious to some. An entire industry of science has developed around the rejection of the claims of natural theology. The once respectable study of God's general revelation in nature has been replaced by the claim that the sign points us nowhere and for no reason. Materialists will incite us to ignore the arrow pointing toward heaven, having us believe instead that even if there were an arrow, it would point nowhere but back toward earth. "Just take nature for what it is," they say, "and stop asking questions of the supernatural."

But whether naturalist or supernaturalist, we need to ask questions concerning the world and our knowledge of it. Inquisitiveness is only natural, even when stifled by the unfortunate presuppositions of both unthinking theists (who shun debate) and ardent atheistic dogmatists (whose "correct" answer concerning origins is that it came from itself).[2] According to the latter, only a moron could miss this self-evident incantation of "truth," or better said, insanity. In a world, God in absentia, there is no other place from which the universe could have come. The theory may change but the conclusion is the same: "It doesn't matter where it came from as long as God had nothing to do with it."

Belligerence, sarcasm, and general antagonism should in no way exemplify all opposition to theism. The world is full of religious skeptics whose honest search for knowledge about our *source* of knowledge yields a more humble acknowledgement: "We are working on it. . . . We have some good theories in place. . . . We may never know." But no matter the motive of the scientific theorist, his theories will come and go and be given a proper hearing in both academia and the media so long as he is careful to presuppose methodological materialism and exclude the possibility of a supernatural being. Do your science, but do not let it lead you toward a Creator. Do your science but do not get any "funny ideas" about God.

Funny ideas about God risk becoming "serious ideas" about God, and these serious ideas risk making theists (or worse, Christians) out of us. But having seen the errors of both skepticism and reliance on unguided human reason, "serious ideas" about God are the clear and reasonable alternative.

---

2. For more on the "it came from itself" argument, see Hawking and Mlodinow, *Grand Design*. For an excellent rebuttal to the "it came from itself" argument, see Lennox, *God and Stephen Hawking*.

Opening the Book of Nature

The uncomfortable interchange between skepticism and rationalism has already led us to abandon both, to conclude that knowledge is possible only because there is a God and to insist that since there is a God, insanity can finally be thrown off and replaced with the hopeful possibility of real knowledge about the universe. But we cannot stop there. This solemn realization about the source of knowledge leads us to the all-the-more significant notion that since there is a God, *knowledge of God* is possible. Since there is a God, knowledge of the universe is not our ultimate goal.

All of the world's knowledge scarcely counts for much if we glibly shrug off its ultimate application, namely, to know God. True knowledge about the world, though a commodity of great value, is at its core a sign pointing to something greater. Natural theology's *deductive arguments* for God's existence serve as theistic proofs interpreted from the signs of nature. Bypassing any reliance on holy books, these proofs attempt to eliminate assumptions, whether for or against God. The *natural theologian* lets the evidence lead him as he begins with what is observed in nature. After constructing solid premises through his appeal to reason and empirical evidence, he may then conclude that nature points to God.

The founders of modern science operated according to a framework of natural theology, letting the evidence lead them. They saw him in the heavens; they saw him in the atoms they studied. God had left his fingerprint (his signature) in everything that can possibly be tested and tried by man. Louis Pasteur, who is perhaps best known for developing pasteurization and the vaccine against rabies (among other things), famously said that "science brings men nearer to God." Science was not an alternative to theism but a means by which theism was vindicated in nature. For Pasteur, nature was a clearly marked panel whose arrow pointed unmistakably to a far greater reality. Men like Pasteur saw the universe as an enormous astronomical clock whose intricacies loudly broadcast the Divine Mind behind their existence.

Others drew similar conclusions. William Paley has inspired generations of theologians, philosophers, and scientists to use deductive arguments as proofs for the existence of God. Paley's arguments by deduction are set out as follows:

1. Based on both scientific and philosophical reflection, we have reason to believe that the universe is created.
2. Anything created must have a creator.
3. Therefore, the universe has a creator.

PART TWO: ASCENT INTO KNOWLEDGE

Included in natural theology's legion of arguments for God's existence are various popular versions of the *moral argument, ontological argument*, and *cosmological argument*. The last of these three has been used to reason for the necessity of a first cause or non-contingent being in the universe. Thomas Aquinas ardently argued for this proof by claiming that a finite entity cannot be the basis of its own existence. It must have a first cause that supports its existence as a finite being. Thomas's intent was to argue both for a being that ranked first among all beings and for a being from which all others were derived.

Leibniz later adapted this argument by appealing to the *principle of sufficient reason*, which states that if something contingent exists, there is a sufficient reason or explanation for its existence, and that this explanation must come either from the necessity of its own existence or from something outside and beyond itself.[3] Since the universe is neither a meaningless unexplained anomaly nor a necessary self-explanatory agent, it must derive its explanation from something that needs no further explanation—something eternal. Only God, therefore, can explain the existence of the universe.

Further uses of the cosmological argument include the Kalam version, developed and first used in the Middle Ages by both Muslim and Christian theologians, to argue for the existence of an Eternal Being. Through the studious work of philosophers like William Lane Craig, the Kalam cosmological argument has seen a tremendous revival and consideration among serious thinkers. In its basic form, it argues . . .

1. All things that begin to exist must have a cause.
2. The universe began to exist.
3. Therefore, the universe must have a cause for its existence.
4. The first and ultimate cause for the universe must, itself, be uncaused.
5. The only possible uncaused cause for the universe is an Eternal Being.

Much excellent work has been done in philosophy in defense of these and other theistic arguments, and my goal is not to repeat the work already done by others in this field. The theistic arguments do not simply point to some vague, impersonal, semi-intelligent mind or minds who have worked out a halfway decent universe. Rather, they point to a being much like that described in the pages of Scripture whose designed plan for the universe has given us an awesome and overwhelmingly detailed world. The conclusions

---

3. See Leibniz, *Monadology*.

of the theistic arguments do not make any assumptions about God that are not already sufficiently allowed for in the premises. Instead, they come together to amplify the reality of an intelligent, creative, omnipotent, and eternal Being who is logically necessary to the existence of this universe.

The unique qualities of the Christian tradition favor its God as the only God who meets the criteria for a first cause. It serves as advantageous to Christianity that there are so few gods in so few religious traditions that meet the qualifications described above. James Sennett has argued that "theism is a preferable alternative to other established religions" in that it (1) benefits from an enormous amount of philosophical scrutiny which has strengthened it, (2) lends itself to the investigation of and response to numerous philosophical problems, and (3) does not suffer from ad hoc formulations.[4]

To clarify, Sennett points out that "throughout two millennia of critical examination and over two hundred years of top flight antagonistic criticism, there have not arisen refutations sufficient to compel all thinking people to reject . . ." theistic belief as a plausible explanation for the universe.[5] No litany has been conclusive enough to shut theism from the minds of thinking people. Furthermore, numerous philosophical conundrums that have popped up in the history of Western thought are properly answered only within the framework of theism. Sennett goes on to say that "one of the most remarkable features of traditional theism is the fact that it can be used to answer so many classical philosophical problems without significant alteration."[6] Naturalistic, polytheistic, and pantheistic belief systems do not adequately explicate morality, human origins, mind, rationality, and the human condition of greatness and wretchedness. Nor are these belief systems adequate in explaining basic human emotions such as love.[7] Finally, theism stands independent of the innumerable philosophical questions developed over centuries of inquiry. Theistic belief is not simply assembled with hast and negligence out of an attempt to respond to philosophical dilemmas. It is, rather, the result of God's revelation as he

---

4. Sennett, "Hume's Stopper," 93.
5. Ibid., 94.
6. Ibid., 94.
7. See Haddad, *Leaving Dirt Place*. Here I argue that when comparing various naturalistic, pantheistic, polytheistic, and theistic belief systems, Christianity is the only worldview that explains the origin of love in a personal God who demonstrated that love through his atoning (saving) sacrifice on the cross.

communicates his divine nature and gracious *salvific* plan for an ignorant and rebellious people.

The revelation of God in nature suggests that the justified true beliefs we hold about the universe serve as a true basis and justification for belief in a Creator-God. At its core, natural theology purports that God can indeed be known even when prior theistic knowledge is lacking. This is why, contrary to the radical empiricists whose study of nature is limited to just that, *natural theologians* believe that nature points beyond nature. British Enlightenment empiricist, John Locke, made this statement:

> The visible marks of extraordinary wisdom and power, appear so plainly in all the works of the creation, that a rational creature, that will but seriously reflect on them, cannot miss the discovery of a *Deity*: and the influence, that the discovery of such a being must necessarily have on the minds of all, that have but once heard of it, is so great, and carries such a weight of thought and communication with it, that it seems stranger to me, that a whole nation of men should be found anywhere so brutish, as to want the notion of God; than that they should be without any notion of numbers, or fire.[8]

Knowledge of God is the ultimate goal. And according to natural theology, God is right there—you can't miss him.[9] Since knowledge about the universe is possible, we cannot help but infer from it certain ideas about God. You might look out into the universe and pretend you did not see him, but according to proponents of natural theology, we all know that is not true. As the cosmological argument shows, God is the logical conclusion reached by our observations. If you do not and cannot see him, it is only because you do not want to.

GOD CLARIFIES NATURE

Throughout the history of thought, religious skeptics have concentrated much of their intellectual energies against natural theology and the conclusions of its deductive arguments, using similar deductive methods to

---

8. Locke, *Essay Concerning Human Understanding*, 95. It must be understood that as an empiricist, Locke did not believe that man has innate knowledge of God or a divine sense. Rather, as the above quote suggests, he advocated observations about nature as a means by which all men have a sense that there is a deity.

9. For a clear and ample treatment of the design and other arguments for the existence of God, see Groothuis, *Christian Apologetics*.

Opening the Book of Nature

uncover weaknesses in the arguments' logic. And while the theistic proofs have been brushed aside by many as rusty relics of ruined medieval monasteries, rigorous maintenance of the arguments and a resurgence of interest in theistic proofs have produced a comprehensive and reasoned defense of a faith that is not easily toppled. The individual proofs for God's existence, when examined carefully, offer tremendous incentive to reconsider a naturalistic interpretation of reality. But though there is strength in these arguments, some theologians prefer a different approach to natural theology, claiming that the universe as a whole must instead be interpreted in light of God. Taking this view, theologian Alister McGrath understands natural theology "as the enterprise of engaging and interpreting nature on the basis of the fundamental beliefs of the Christian tradition."[10] By this, he means that observable nature affirms that "the fundamental themes of the Christian faith offer the best explanation for what is seen."[11] So rather than a sign pointing to God, we have a theistic lens that gives a coherent picture of reality as a whole.

The observer of nature will bring with him certain presuppositions as he gazes into his telescope or jots down equations on paper. He will assume a particular worldview while measuring oceanic currents or dissecting and documenting the innards of beasts. Remember that he is insane and prone to introduce any number of erroneous ideas into his scientific system. But from the lunatic's den, some few "fools" have stumbled into the light and realized that if they are to trust any scientific conclusions, this will happen only within a theistic worldview. Having recovered at least a few of their lost marbles, they are able to recognize that the universe as a whole makes sense only when interpreted through the lens of theism.

Biology may be interpreted through the spectacles of blind unthinking evolution, as might geology, or any other science. But we are not looking just at biology or geology. A true and believable worldview must explain neurological functions, behaviors, emotions, psychological states, morality, relationships, evil, time, space, mathematics, and beyond. It must explain each of these individually. It must explain them as an interconnected total.

---

10. McGrath, *Fine Tuned Universe*, 20. While some of McGrath's ideas on natural theology are useful, a word of caution should be issued to his rejection of "proofs" for the Christian faith. McGrath can be disparaging at times toward the highly developed and logically sound deductive arguments for the existence of God that have been employed by thoughtful Christians for centuries. His apologetic method is summarized in McGrath, *Mere Apologetics*.

11. Ibid., 20.

PART TWO: ASCENT INTO KNOWLEDGE

It must account for the whole of time and space and everything contained therein.

Inductive natural theology does not observe design in nature, *per se*. Rather, it observes nature alone and infers from nature both design and a Designer as the best possible explanation.[12] McGrath lays out this reasoning as follows:

1. There is order in the universe, or various universes, for which human beings are not ultimately responsible.

2. The best explanation of this observation is the existence of a transcendent cause or order.

3. The "cause" has bestowed upon us the cognitive powers required for observing evidences of it and for inferring from these its continuing efficacy.[13]

Belief in the God who grants and substantiates human justified true beliefs is the best explanation for everything we know about the natural world. And what we know about the natural world has the explanatory power to point us back to God. It only makes sense that the God who lies at the source of our knowledge of the world is the end to which our knowledge of the world leads. Without God, we cannot have knowledge, and without knowledge we cannot know God. In this way, God gives us our knowledge so that our knowledge can give us God.

This may seem circular, but the argument from knowledge and the arguments of natural theology converge after arriving from two different points of departure. The deductive arguments of natural theology are telling us that nature points to God's existence. At the same time, by explaining knowledge of the world in light of God's existence, we can trust our knowledge-building faculties to lead us to the acceptance of natural theology in the first place.

Arguments fueled by induction allow the observer acquaintance with the copious evidence for the Designer of the natural world.[14] The design inference evoked here is rooted in God-given cognitive capacities that best explain the universe. The arguments are not, according to Douglas

---

12. Ibid., 30.

13. Ibid., 43. See also Peirce, *Collected Papers*, 6:495–7.

14. For more on the design argument, see Swinburne, "Teleological Arguments." See also Meyer, *Signature in the Cell*. Through his study of the cell, Meyer lays out a thorough case in support of an Intelligent Designer behind the existence and structure of DNA.

Groothuis, "based on *ignorance* about the natural world but on *knowledge* about it."[15] Proponents of *design inference* propose that the natural world is not the result of either chance or natural laws and that knowledge of this world is best explained by the Designer at its source. The inductive argument from knowledge states the following:

1. Justified true beliefs are only possible when human cognitive apparatuses can be guaranteed to function properly and when the universe is designed to account for objective truth.

2. The existence of God best guarantees the proper function of our cognitive faculties and best allows for the existence of objective truth.

3. Therefore, God exists.

As concluded here, the universe is *best* explained by God. And as we have concluded earlier in this book, the human capacity to know is explained *only* by God. Without a designed plan and purpose behind the human mind, knowledge would be impossible. Before you so much as expend an ounce of mental energy to reflect on an idea and make a knowledge-claim, you are already assuming God's existence. Without God, there is no possibility of knowing anything. Natural theology complements this idea by claiming that by knowing anything, we risk, for better or worse, discovering our Creator all the more. But we risk more than that. We risk being awakened from the comfortable insanity that drives us to deny our Creator, deny ourselves, and deny our world so as to continue scratching out a chaotic existence in a universe devoid of reason.

We should be willing to admit that if there is no God, Darwin's theory is the most coherent explanation we can assemble on our origins. If there is no God, we have to come up with something that explains us to ourselves. But explaining madness to a madman is hardly a satisfying solution. Darwin has given us a universe in which we can know nothing. He has given us a universe where beliefs can never be justified and where skepticism reigns. Conversely, God has given us a universe in which we might know him, and in knowing him, know countless other truths.

The evidence written so clearly in the *Book of Nature* should lead us to the same "immense conclusion" pondered by William Paley centuries ago, "that there is a God; a perceiving, intelligent, designing Being; at the head of creation, and from whose will it proceeded."[16] Likewise, the *Book of Nature*

---

15. Groothuis, *Christian Apologetics*, 247.
16. Paley, *Natural Theology*, 230.

PART TWO: ASCENT INTO KNOWLEDGE

should lead us with Jonathan Edwards to hear God's "voice" in his work—a voice that instructs intelligent beings in knowledge of their Creator.[17] This is a more satisfying and altogether saner approach to science than to say, "It doesn't matter where it came from as long as God had nothing to do with it."

BOOK OF NATURE, BOOK OF GOD

God is the conclusion that most naturally fits the evidence, and this itself is evidenced in history. The development of natural theology, as it is known today, can rightly be credited to long-dead theologians with a highly developed enthusiasm for inference, but natural theology itself is an ancient idea not unknown to the writers of Scripture. Genesis 1:27 tells us that God created man in his own image so that man could share in the creative capacities, rationality, and intelligence of his Creator. If God is at the origin of man, it is only reasonable that man's cognitive capacities will cause him to habitually stumble back toward his Creator. King David understood this when he announced in one of his Psalms:

> The heavens declare the glory of God; the skies proclaim the works of his hands. Day after day they pour forth speech; night after night they display knowledge. (Ps. 19:1–2)

The silent, inanimate, and distant stars speak despite themselves, and the message they proclaim is one of an "immense conclusion": *God is there*. The brilliant swirling expanse of the night sky that teems with stars, nebula, galaxies, black holes, and countless other phenomena that David could have only imagined testifies to something beyond itself. No lesser response will do. To simply say that "there might be some sort of a god out there somewhere" is hardly a message worth proclaiming. What David proclaimed is that God must absolutely be at the origin of the universe. It is doubtful that he was a great scientist in any modern sense of the word, but in looking to the heavens, David saw exactly what God intended for him to see. Through his theistic lens, David could see and understand the cosmos.

The man Job, even in his suffering and misery, reminded his friends as he sat among the ashes, clothed in sackcloth and covered in sores, that God alone is Maker of heaven and earth—the One who formed the earth and gave life and meaning to each and every thing contained within it (Job

---

17. Edwards, *Images of Divine Things*, 61.

9:8–10). This was self-evident. Who had laid the foundations of the earth? Who had fashioned the stars and set the dimensions of the seas? Who clothed the earth in clouds and made light to illuminate its beauty? Who made the water cycle to clean and refresh the earth? Who used starlight to paint a fresco across the night sky (Job 38)? There is no doubt that Job knew the answers. He knew the earth beneath his feet and the sky above his head. He knew exactly who was at its source.

Had Job ceded to doubt, as to post-Enlightenment sensibilities, when faced with God's litany of questions, things might not have turned out so well for him. Had he squeaked out the latest fashionable answer to come marching down the catwalk—"I think it came from itself . . . moron"—we might have a very different conclusion to the book of Job than what we read today. Job was right to go with the obvious. He was right to understand the world in light of its Creator.

Incidentally, self-proclaimed theists are not the only ones expected to arrive at the conclusions of David and Job. The first chapter of Paul's epistle to the Romans states rather bluntly that God exists, and like it or not, you know it:

> For since the creation of the world, God's invisible qualities—his eternal power and divine nature—have been clearly seen, being understood from what has been made, so that men are without excuse. For although they knew God, they neither glorified him as God nor gave thanks to him, but their thinking became futile and their foolish hearts were darkened. (Rom. 1:20–21)

Too often we welcome knowledge but lament the natural movement of knowledge toward its actual source, curtailing it so as to prohibit it from telling us anything we may not want to hear. Pascal rightly noted that "we run heedlessly into the abyss after putting something in front of us to stop us seeing it."[18] But if we open our eyes to knowledge, we will be led toward the God who, as John Calvin put it, stamped knowledge of the Divine on "the breasts of all men."[19]

Knowledge of God is printed legibly upon the human conscience like a sixth sense, the *sensus divinitatis*. Calvin said it so eloquently:

> All men of sound judgment will therefore hold, that a sense of deity is indelibly engraved on the human heart. And that this belief is

---

18. Pascal, *Pensées*, 166/183, 53.
19. Calvin, *Institutes*, (I–3), sec. 3.

naturally engendered in all, and thoroughly fixed as it were in our very bones, is strikingly attested by the contumacy of the wicked, who, though they struggle furiously, are unable to extricate themselves from the fear of God.[20]

In agreement with Calvin, John Frame says this of God: "He does not wait passively for us to discover Him, but He makes himself known."[21] Creation is the voice of God reminding us to put on our theistic spectacles and look again at his magnificent work.

But the dead horse need not be beaten. By now we have seen that natural theology affords us a perfectly plausible description of the ways in which our knowledge of the world gives rise to knowledge of our Creator. The Knowledge-Giver has given us knowledge of his presence, and this knowledge is adequate enough to whet our appetites for more.

THE LIMITS OF NATURAL THEOLOGY

Knowledge of nature gives us knowledge of its Creator. However, inasmuch as nature gives, there is much more hidden from our senses. The knowledge given to us by nature does not sufficiently satisfy our desire for relationship with God. Though we have received certain general revelations about God, these, unfortunately, are prone to two glaring inadequacies that necessitate the precision of further revelation. *The first damper placed on the possibility of truly knowing God through nature is found in the communicative limitations from which nature intrinsically suffers.* Nature lacks the vocabulary necessary to fully explain God. A road sign with an arrow and the words "The Moon" printed on it gives a motorist reason to believe that the moon is somewhere and that it can be visited, but it does not mean that the moon is accessible, at least not without additional means to get there. Knowledge of the world may very well point us to God, but knowledge of the world does not allow us to know God relationally.

We have already chased knowledge down rabbit trails that have led us to insanity. Countless scientists have gone missing in the black hole of speculation after running heedlessly off the edges of various epistemic cliffs, their white lab coats disappearing into the fog below. In trying to explain reality, our endless theories lead us further from it. We are lured into

---

20. Ibid., 10.
21. Frame, *Doctrine of Knowledge*, 42.

Opening the Book of Nature

invisible worlds where we are guided more by imagination than by truth and where the specter of speculation is our only link back to the real world.

The real world is a strange one indeed where the sun appears to move ever so slowly from horizon to horizon. In the real world people eat, drink, and laugh. Others suffer from hunger and cold. Distant clouds wisp in the high blue heavens. Conversations hum in the air like bees. If the earth were really round, no one would ever know it simply by looking out their window. There are people with needs, others with fears, and those with joys to be expressed. The carpenter works his lumber. The farmer sows his seed. The fisherman casts his nets. The mother nurses her child. The mathematician makes his calculation. The madman rages. The world that matters most is the one in which people, locked in a paradox of greatness and misery, need knowledge that will allow them to answer life's ultimate questions. In the real world there is a God who is the Source of human knowledge and the Ultimate End of human knowledge.

We can know reality no better than to know these simple things. These are the justified true beliefs by which we live. The knowable world is the world into which we are born and from which we depart. It is a world in which we—the practitioners of life—labor to gain more and more knowledge until it is washed away by death. We pass this knowledge on, others add to it, and if it has some practical value we pursue it even further, but if not, it is forgotten. In speculating over the minuscule and guessing about the grand, we ignore the actual. Rather than bringing us closer to reality, our inquiry often takes us further from it. We chase quarks through the infinitesimal micro-world only to discover something smaller still—something that does not exist, but could, and should, and might if only we keep on looking. Sure, we might learn something, but the quarks themselves will never tell us why we long for knowledge or how we attain it. We can gaze billions of light-years through space at the formation of a star only to find another older, farther, astronomical oddity—something that leads us to wonder if maybe our universe is actually a small part of something larger still, or a drop in an infinite multiverse that does not really exist, but could, and should, and might if only we keep up our speculation. Again, we might learn much by looking to the stars, but we will never know the reality of the inner condition of greatness and wretchedness that vies for control over our miserable lives. We can muster our intellectual forces to invent communication machines that open us to a whole new digital universe at the cost of losing contact with the very people who stand an arm's length away. But despite all this, we continue to focus on the subsidiary, distracting ourselves from the most real of realities.

Nature (the sign that points to God) has become for the atheist a god in and of itself. By looking to nature as a means by which to bury God once and for all, a new and lesser god has taken form only to divert our knowledge from the right conclusions to the wrong ones. But atheists are not the only ones to misunderstand the message of nature. Theists blunder when they make God's general revelation a sufficient condition for relational knowledge of him. By knowing nature, they too risk thinking they have achieved sufficient knowledge of their Creator. But this is not what nature gives us. The wonders of nature can only take us so far. Within every living thing, tiny factories, countless in number and invisible to the human eye, are efficiently constructing the world of life that surrounds us and in which we ourselves share. My scientist friends tell me that I am made of tissue, which is, in turn, made of cells. These, I am told, are made of organelles, which are made of molecules, which are made of atoms. The minuteness of the world is enough to leave nearly anyone overwhelmed by its wonder. All this points us to God, but it, in and of itself, is not God. Natural theology may allow us to *know of God* by our reason and by our senses, but natural theology will never allow us the intimate knowledge of God that only comes by true relationship with him. Natural theology takes us to the right door but does not allow the latch to be opened.

But the limits of God's general revelation in nature are not the only obstruction to true knowledge of the Divine. *The second damper placed on the possibility of knowing God can be attributed to none other than our own spiritual blindness.* Though God gave us the capacity to function properly, we have broken ourselves. Our damaged lives and fragmented minds are unable to work quite right. Rebellion against God is the culprit and because of this sin, the sinless God has withdrawn himself from us, meaning that we cannot, by our own effort, attain knowledge of him. This knowledge-abating, death-inducing, love-defiling sin is defined by theologian Wayne Grudem as "any failure to conform to the moral law of God in act, attitude, or manner."[22] Sin is any offense committed against the righteous law of God.

Christians often forget just how pervasive sin can be. Its ubiquitous poisoning of creation extends far beyond moral depravity, encapsulating the degeneration of our physical bodies and our noetic capacities. We are right to be sensitive to the reality that "sin motivates fallen people to distort

---

22. Grudem, *Systematic Theology*, 490.

the truth, to flee from it, to exchange it for a lie, and to misuse it."[23] This has been evident from the very beginning.

The events of Genesis 3 are significant enough that we must return there once again. We have already deliberated on the acts of Adam and Eve as the first skeptics, who doubted the very realities that should have been more than evident to them. We have already considered Adam and Eve as the first rationalists, who attempted epistemic certainty by their own efforts when enticed by the possibility of absolute moral knowledge. We have seen that our first parents were true epistemologists, concerned with what could and should be known. But these first "philosophers" must, above all else, be remembered as the first image-bearers of God who fell into sin by their disobedience. The first man was the hallmark of God's creation. His wife Eve was a woman formed by the hand of God—doubtless a woman of great intellectual capacity and surpassing beauty. But when these two disobeyed the one command given them by God, sin was invited into the world and creation was scarred both physically and morally. Beauty faded and the mind became susceptible to unceasing error. Our parents were driven, raving mad and miserable, from the presence of God to fade away in isolation from their Creator and to propagate the current race of madmen.

Man, in all of his greatness, may still be the apex of creation, but his greatness has been marred by the guilt he carries with him. By his rebellion against the perfections of a holy God, man has fallen into the doom of guilt and death (Rom. 5:12–21). The probational moral freedom given to Adam and Eve in the Garden of Eden was ultimately abused and used to usurp God's gracious gifts of honor, moral goodness, and a relational knowledge of God (Gen. 3; Ps. 8:4–8). In their lust for more of these good things, our first parents, having succumbed to the wiles of the devil, disobeyed God and made a mockery of his grace, bringing his wrath upon the very race that Adam and Eve themselves represented. As a result, we who are organically bound to the race of man suffer from the paradox of its glory and wretchedness. Mankind, as a family, carries the burden of this sin from one generation to the next (Rom. 3:10–18). We sin, thus, because we are already doomed sinners, choosing always to rebel against our Creator. The poison of sin has permeated our race and has left us hopelessly ruined. Diminished and deposed, we wander the earth estranged and cursed, perpetually prohibited from knowing our God.

---

23. Frame, *Doctrine of Knowledge*, 20. See also Romans 1:25, 28.

PART TWO: ASCENT INTO KNOWLEDGE

The curse of sin has affected our freedom and removed our ability to do what is right. We are immersed in such depravity that apart from God's grace, we lack all desire to seek God and practice righteousness. Apart from God's grace, what moral freedom we have moves us always toward ruin. Our sin has restricted both our moral volition and our intellectual capacity, leaving us bound to folly. Our will is so corrupt that we deceive ourselves into thinking we are free even as we are bound helplessly to the slavery of sin (John 8:34). Though God's existence guarantees our ability to possess knowledge, our knowledge does not guarantee our ability to know God. This is the logical result of the sin that, like a poison dripped in our ears, drives us to delusions about the Divine.[24]

The posterity left to us by our first parents is one of intellectual insanity. The *Westminster Confession of Faith* reminds us of this:

> By this sin they fell from their original righteousness and communion with God, and so became dead in sin, and wholly defiled in all the faculties and parts of soul and body.[25]

Because of sin, our beliefs became incoherent and disorganized, lacking justification while confounding truth. The brilliance of human minds became dull, and knowledge became repugnant to the transgressors who, without restraint, lusted for incredulity. The intellectual posterity of sin is none other than epistemic confusion. Grudem points out the effects of sin on human rational faculties:

> All sin is ultimately irrational. It really did not make sense for Satan to rebel against God in the expectation of being able to exalt himself above God. Nor did it make sense for Adam and Eve to think that there could be any gain is disobeying the words of their Creator. These were foolish choices.[26]

These were no less than the choices of madmen deceived by folly. As an "organic whole" the human race carries the malignancy of sin as blinders over our eyes, preventing us from seeing our Creator with clarity and knowing him eternally.[27]

---

24. The material in this and the previous paragraph was adapted from an unpublished EFCA ordination paper, "Doctrinal Thesis" by Jonah Haddad.
25. *Westminster Confession of Faith*, article 6.
26. Grudem, *Systematic Theology*, 493.
27. Ibid., 493.

Natural theology has given us knowledge of God, but this knowledge is still obscured by the limitations of human finitude and by the cloak of sin that blinds our eyes. Natural theology has done great things for us by pointing us to our Creator and giving us a lens by which to view the world, but we would be fools to think that this alone is enough to restore us to a true and saving knowledge of our Lord. The knowledge obtained by natural theology is only enough to bring us to some awkward place between sanity and madness where we, like medieval court jesters, dance about in outlandish hats and clumsy shoes, the toes of which curl up at the ends with little bells attached that jingle as we juggle and rhyme and make music with various parts of our scrawny bodies. Natural theology is not enough to take the fool out of us or to drive away the last of our reluctant lunacy.

Our study of the universe tells us much, but more than anything, it proclaims the vast depths of our overwhelming and multidimensional ignorance about many things, including God. Failing to fully know the universe, we subsequently fail to know ourselves, who are part of it. If we cannot know the physical realities that would seem so evident to us, how could we ever hope to know the spiritual realities that lie at the core of all reality? We need something more than what nature alone can give us. *We need God.*

9

The Beginning of Knowledge

HECTIC, ORGANISMIC PANDEMONIUM PRESSES heavily against the streets, burning impressions into the mind of a silent spectator who sits deliberating. He studies the crowded urban chaos at an outdoor café table. With anonymity, he slips cognitively into the cityscape, sipping and staring, digesting and discerning the moving masses that make up the ever-constant columns of people. With pendulous motion, appendages move in measured increments upon the walkways. In measured time, the measured masses charge the beleaguered city and then retreat back from the routines of business in the ebb and flow of urban life. The observer sits and studies the world around him, gaining knowledge all the while, but even this is only partial.

As the observer continues to watch, the crowd disassembles into unique sentient beings. Our spectator sees them clearly: black-suited automatons of the skillfully wielded cigarette; ambulatory veterans of the bum leg; procurers of the avant-garde—the attachéd, the mumblers, and the dazed, each dispatched to a destination of his own. Many others glance nervously or stroll along carefree, their complexions laid bare, warts and all. Our vigilant and discerning witness points to the massive tapestry of life: the woof and the warp of the wealthy and the impoverished, the drugged and the lucid, the successful and the fruitless, the peaceful and the anxious, and the joyful and the melancholy. The faces of beauty and ugliness span the spectrum. And while much is made visible, even more remains impervious to the ocular penetrations of our witness. He cannot truly know the hearts and minds of those he observes.

The Beginning of Knowledge

If you, as an observer, know how to decode the signs flashed unknowingly before your eyes, you will gain certain *justified true beliefs* about each of these people. You will get to know them, albeit only partially. Come back day after day, and you may start to recognize the same faces, same gestures, and same moods. You might come to know their routines and their tastes, but you will never know more than the merely superficial unless they choose to reveal it to you. You will never know what they know. You will never know their fears or secrets, pains, joys, or madness. You will never truly know any of them unless they draw back the curtains and let you glimpse into their minds. A little at a time, their discreet disclosures will prove that some justified true beliefs must be revealed.

Much like the knowledge of God and his universe attained by natural theology, your knowledge of the crowds, gleaned by observation, is still only a product of your limited intellectual capacities and attentiveness to detail. A person's interests and emotional state may be guessed with more or less accuracy as you observe his posture, his gestures, or his manner of dress, but the content of his heart, mind, and soul will never be gathered unless he is plucked from the crowd and invited into conversation. Once his tongue is loosed, verbal communications will begin to flow. Piece by piece the revelations that pour from him will gradually assemble themselves into a clearer image.

Revelation of this kind depends wholly on the willingness of the discloser, so that the formerly translucent becomes increasingly transparent. As we have seen, the study of natural theology trains our eyes to see the general revelations of God and to recognize him as he moves about the crowd. Eyes that remain open will enjoy a glimpse of his glory, but there is more to him than this, and unless he comes to us and speaks, too much of him will remain forever hidden from our sight. Unless he comes to us through divine disclosure, the wonders of his mind will forever elude us. Unless we go further than ourselves to apprehend our God, we will be forever lost.[1]

But praise be to God, for spoken he has! Through prophets and apostles and from the mouths of peasants and monarchs alike, he has spoken to our forefathers at many times and in various ways (Heb. 1:1). He has given us the riches of the words of Scripture, and better still, has revealed the fullness of his glory and redemptive plan in Christ, the Word made flesh (John 1:14). A greater knowledge than anything we could ever imagine has

---

1. Calvin, *Institutes*, (I–5), sec. 3.

PART TWO: ASCENT INTO KNOWLEDGE

come to us through his *special revelation*. And where man's intellect ends, a different and greater Mind has spoken wisdom into the void of human knowledge. Through his special revelation (his direct communication with man through prophetic words and the advent of Jesus), the eternal God has brought healing to the insanity of the fallen, finite, and fettered mind of man.

His special revelation is the key to overcoming the madness that distorts reality and tyrannizes justified true belief. God's special revelation is far greater than any knowledge of him we could ever hope to attain ourselves because the riches of this revelation are based, not on what our finite and corrupt minds hopelessly seek to understand, but on what the eternal and holy God of the universe has chosen to reveal. The knowledge made available to us through God's special revelation is founded in an internally coherent divine conversation that spans recipients, languages, epochs, and geographical locations. God has invited himself into conversation with humanity whether we like it or not and has unveiled words that are living, active, and more than capable of awakening us from our insanity (Heb. 4:12).

SPECIAL REVELATION: THE WORD MADE TEXT

The uniqueness of the Christian faith is in its twofold special revelation: the *Word made text* and the *Word made flesh*. The Word made text, or Bible, is the accumulation of divine correspondence with humanity, revealed progressively to various prophets yet unified by a central focus on the nature, character, and salvific work of God. The task of the Bible is to convey proper knowledge about God so man can correctly understand his own existence, his spiritual condition, and his relationship to God. As a God-centered book, the *Word made text* speaks to the reality of God's special revelation in Christ Jesus: the *Word made flesh*.

It is not possible here to even scratch the surface of the voluminous body of scholarly work that has served to demonstrate the facts of Jesus' earthly sojourn. Neither is it practical to reproduce all the research that has been done in favor of the accurate transmission of God's Word from the original texts to the copies of the originals that we now use to realize various modern translations. The focus of such research is to emphasize the factuality of time and space events that are crucial to both human history and human eternity by delineating arguments in favor of the historical narratives and prophetic claims of Scripture.[2] Further arguments seek to elucidate why the biblical *canon*, or collection of sacred writings, was not hastily constructed by a handful of sinister men, bereft of scruples and prone to deception. The canon emerged, rather, out of writings that contained a coherent message, early circulation in the churches, and nearly unanimous recognition by the primitive church as having been written under apostolic and prophetic authority as attested to by Christ and the apostles (Luke 24:44; John 5:39; 16:12–13; Gal. 1–2; 2 Pet. 1:20–21).[3]

The importance of the research concerning the historical reliability of Scripture and the life of Jesus (including his resurrection) cannot be overstated. But our concern henceforth will lie in a different set of questions. In seeking a reliable foundation for knowledge, we have already procured the solid surface (the necessity of God) on which to build the rest. Since God must exist as the Source of knowledge, we can rightly reason that he conveys knowledge to us, for a being who lies at the source of knowledge must certainly want to enjoy a reciprocal knowledge of his creation. However, what might confuse and even trouble us is the startling surplus of so-called divine revelations issued by every religious prognosticator under the sun. But rather than dismantle and evaluate every seemingly divine dissertation printed to date, we will simply explore the uniqueness of special revelation in the Christian theological tradition by inquiring into how this revelation is of eternal importance to all men.

Have you seen such men—hunch-shouldered yet astute—pouring over musty holy books in near monastic meditation as they inquire of the eternal God? There they sit in silence, eyes fixed on the text below, minds lifted toward God's resplendent glory. They know the limits of human knowledge. They know that if ultimate reality is to be known, the Source of knowledge himself must make it known. They are not ruled by crushing Pyrrhonian doubts or inflated rationalistic self-surety. They trust that knowledge of the world is possible and that their common sense realism will take them to the limits of knowledge, but not beyond. And so they look to their Creator and the truths he discloses.

Each word of Scripture points us toward *the* Word: Christ. Each word of Scripture says something about God and our relationship to him that we

---

2. For more on the historical reliability of the Bible, and particularly the New Testament see Blomberg, *Historical Reliability*. See also Stott, *Authority of the Bible*.

3. For an excellent discussion of the origin of the biblical canon, see Metzger, *Canon of the New Testament*, and Bruce, *Canon of Scripture*. See also Carson and Woodbridge, *Hermeneutics, Authority, and Canon*.

would otherwise never discover on our own.[4] Throughout history, servants of the Lord have understood this, imploring their God to teach them his ways that they might know him more (Exod. 33:12–13). They have publically beseeched him to instruct them in his Word that they might have knowledge of God (Ps. 119:66–67). They have expressed their love for his revelation, proclaiming its flawlessness (2 Sam. 22:31). They have voiced their daily need for biblical sustenance as a vital victual for life (Deut. 8:3).

The follower of Christ sees God's revealed Word as a lamp to his feet and light to his path (Ps. 119:105). He understands that God communicates through propositions of truth that can be accessed, studied, argued, and believed. The follower of Christ understands that this revelation is not to be distorted for his own purpose, but that it exists so that the church would be built up in knowledge of God (2 Cor. 4:2; Eph. 4:13). This is why the apostle Paul prayed so fervently for the Christians at Ephesus, asking that the eyes of their hearts would be enlightened so they might *know* the wonders of the works of God in bringing them to salvation (Eph. 1:17–18). This is why the apostle Luke insisted that his gospel account was written so that his readers would *know* with certainty the truth of Jesus' life, death, and resurrection.

We may rightly agree with Wayne Grudem's assessment that the Bible is "the form of God's Word that is available for study, for public inspection, for repeated examination, and as a basis for mutual discussion."[5] We may further agree that the Bible is more than a literary curiosity of antiquity. The Bible, says Grudem, "points us to the Word of God as a person, namely Jesus Christ, whom we do not now have present in bodily form on earth."[6] The entire focus of Scripture is on something far greater than itself. If we claim to know any god who has not revealed himself to us, then we have done nothing but claim to know a thoroughly unknowable god. Unless God reveals himself to us, we will only accommodate great error about him, about his nature, and about his relationship to us. Pascal comments that "without Scripture, whose only object is Christ, we know nothing, and can see nothing but obscurity and confusion in the nature of God and in nature itself."[7] Calvin adds that "error never can be eradicated from the heart of man until the true knowledge of God has been implanted in it."[8] Calvin's

---

4. See Frame, *Doctrine of the Word*.
5. Grudem, *Systematic Theology*, 50.
6. Ibid., 50.
7. Pascal, *Pensées*, 417/548; 121.
8. Calvin, *Institutes*, (I-6), sec. 3.

reasoning makes perfect sense both biblically and logically. The expulsion of error pays off heartily when the storerooms of the mind are restocked with intellectually satisfying provisions contributed by the glorious grace of God by his revelation in Scripture.

Much can be said about the Bible's literary and historical value alone, but insofar as the epistemic content is concerned, God's revelation in Scripture has been divided into two distinct but congruent volumes: the Old and the New Testaments.[9] The aim of the Old Testament writings is to explain God's purpose and plan for the salvation of a corrupt humanity by pointing God's people to a Savior who had not yet come. The purpose of the New Testament writings is to further elucidate that divine purpose and plan for the salvation of a corrupt humanity by pointing God's people to a Savior who had come but was no longer physically present. In some sense, the Scriptures are physically with us because God the Son, Jesus Christ, is not.

Like the man who sits and watches the buzzing urban commotion, so also will the observer of the universe learn much about his world. Our observer will learn much but not everything. Despite his best efforts, he will know nothing of the wonders of the gospel of God's saving grace in Jesus apart from Scripture and will never hope to grow in his knowledge of God apart from this special revelation (Rom. 10:13–17). The Word made text is necessary, and its necessity in matters of salvific knowledge is further corroborated by its sufficiency in communicating precisely what God intended to transmit and nothing more (Deut. 4:2; Prov. 30:5–6; Rev. 22:18–19). Where Scripture is silent on peripheral or secondary issues, we are left to rational reflection or even guesswork in ascertaining the best response. This is permissible so long as speculation does not morph into man-made dogma. The conclusions drawn by our reflections may serve to clarify our understanding of difficult matters untouched by Scripture, but these man-made clarifications cannot be known with the same surety as those revealed by God himself.

Many religions claim to give us insight into the realities of the world, both physical and spiritual, through divine words in textual form, but only Christianity gives us a word from God that details our need for *the* Word of God, Jesus Christ. Indeed, central to the *Word made text* is its insistence on knowledge of the *Word made flesh*. The uniqueness of the Christian

---

9. The content of both the Old and New Testaments is centered on teaching about God's salvific plan for the redemption of his people by grace through faith. The advantage of those living in a post-New Testament era is that they are able to see the coherency of Old Testament prophecies and foreshadowings of the Messiah come to pass.

PART TWO: ASCENT INTO KNOWLEDGE

Scriptures is its assertion that truth is not restricted to mere propositions or knowledge-claims about this thing or that, but that truth is contained in the very nature of God and embodied in the very person of Jesus.

SPECIAL REVELATION: THE WORD MADE FLESH

Scripture tells the story of the triune God: Father, Son, and Holy Spirit. It tells us of his attributes—his infinite knowledge, his supreme power, his holiness, justice, mercy, and love. It tells us of our estrangement from God through sin. It illuminates us to the insanity that sends us running frenzied from God's presence, offended by his copious love, hands over our ears, so as not to hear rumors of his abounding grace. Scripture tells us that old story of creation, fall, and redemption. It speaks of God's glory, a raging flame and consuming fire, and incites us to cast ourselves down in terror and repentance. It points us to the cross where our God atoned for our sins by substituting himself in our place. What other perfectly innocent man could possibly pay the penalty for transgressors by being so brutally fixed to a cross than Christ himself: the Son, the *Word made flesh* (John 1:1; 14).

Without the coming of Jesus into this world, and without his death and resurrection, our knowledge of God would be disastrously lacking. Yes, we would still have a casual knowledge *of* God through general revelation. Yes, we would still have some knowledge *about* God through his special revelation in Scripture. But without Christ himself, we would have no object to which all of Scripture points. It was by Christ's death on the cross that our debt of sin was paid to a holy God, who would not otherwise tolerate a sinful humanity in his presence and who would not otherwise let himself be known—*truly* known.

To know *of* someone is to know that they exist and little more. To know *about* someone takes your knowledge to a further intermediary place but still lacks the intimacy of relationship. General revelation affords us knowledge of God's existence and activity in the universe. Special revelation in Scripture gives us much knowledge about God and his dealings with man. But until we receive the Word made flesh and come to know him, we will always be hopelessly banished from God's presence.

We can all relate to this in various ways by our relationships with others. Before I was married, I knew *of* my wife because I had heard her name and seen her at a distance. I began to know *about* her after a few exchanges of polite conversation. But it was not until I had spent hour upon hour with

The Beginning of Knowledge

her in deep discussion, understanding her past and sharing her present, that I began to truly know her and love her. In the same way, we can amass tremendous knowledge about God, but until we meet the Word made flesh, we will always be missing something.

And who is this Word made flesh, this God-man? How can a word have body? Who is this divine *Logos*, who though God in nature, humbled himself and lived as a man (Phil. 2:5–11)?[10] The mere mention of a divine Logos, or Word made flesh, incites images of paradox, metaphysical mischief, and esoteric roguery. But this peculiar name—the Word made flesh—reminds us that the message of truth originating in God was, and is, so tightly knit to his character and nature that the two are indissolubly one. He is the eternal God, the Creator of heaven and earth, who adjoined himself to man and lived among us (John 1:1, 14). He speaks the truth because he embodies truth (John 14:6; 18:37–38). He is the only one by whom fallen human beings can know the one true and living God (John 17:3). In Christ (the Word made flesh) is hidden all the riches of knowledge and wisdom about God and this world (Col. 2:2–3).

One of the defining characteristics of Christian theism is that it alone allows God to truly be known through Jesus Christ. No other philosophy or religion accounts for knowledge of the world or knowledge of God because no other belief system calls for the worship of a God who makes himself personally known. Though the monotheistic religions (including Christianity) claim to bring man close to God by offering salvation, only one of them can accomplish this task. Though all of them claim restoration of the fallen human condition, all but one of them fail, for all but one are missing the all-important Christ.

There are three truths concerning the nature of God and the nature of man that are so nearly self-evident that one hardly needs to generate any polemic on their behalf. These three truths are proof enough that man needs more than a mere text that speaks of God. Man is in need of God himself, the Originator of knowledge.

The first of these truths is simply this: *God is holy* (Lev. 11:44–45; 19:2; 1 Pet. 1:16).[11] This means that he is set apart from lesser things. He is morally "other" than his fallen creatures. There is no moral depravity in him by

---

10. The Greek word "logos" literally means "word" but can refer to that which is rational, intellectual, or reasonable. For a good treatment of the concept of the logos in the context of Greek and early Christian thought, see chapters four and five of Holmes, *Fact, Value, and God*.

11. See Sproul, *Holiness of God*.

which to contest the perfection of his goodness and righteousness. God's honor and glory are attached to the moral quality of his holiness, which is a non-negotiable attribute of God, tied to his very being. For God to be God in any monotheistic sense of the term, he must by necessity be holy.

The holiness of God is aptly contrasted with a second truth: *Man is unholy* (Rom. 3:9–18). His best efforts at moral purity are like filthy rags in the sight of a perfect God because no matter the good found in man, he is still born with a corrupt moral nature and susceptible to the nefarious allure of sin (Isa. 64:6). No man who has ever walked this earth is immune to the realities of moral deprivation. Whether we erroneously view good and evil as illusory or whether we falsely consider these categories culturally relative hardly changes the brute fact that man produces his fair share of foul behaviors. If you are honest, you will recognize that the mind of man is overflowing with unholiness. Avarice, dishonesty, egoism, and lust are daily realities with which we struggle, these being perhaps the mildest of our vices. Nonetheless, the Bible calls these things sin. There is little need to further convince ourselves of the litany we already know to exist. One thing is certain, whether in thought or in deed, our sins have made us unholy. No one can justly claim to possess the perfections of the holiness of God.

This fact, when added to the content of the first, divulges our third and final truth: *The holiness of God and the utter lack of holiness in man are a devastating combination.* And here is where the heart of the problem is to be found. Moral filth and the ugliness of sin have no place in the presence of a holy God. As it is, there can be no relationship between God and man. If we can imagine the degree to which we are all repulsed by the sight and stench of a festering cadaver, we can likewise imagine the extent to which God must, by nature of his holiness, be repulsed by our festering sin. And if we can imagine the grief we might experience on finding that the corpse is that of a dear friend or beloved family member, we can then image the grief God feels at the sight of his beloved creatures who are now dead in sin. Our moral delinquency has made a separation between us and God—a separation that leaves a gaping hole in our knowledge of all things both natural and supernatural (Isa. 59:2). John Stott says it well: "If human beings have sinned (which they have), and if they are responsible for their sins (which they are), then they are guilty before God."[12] In other words, human beings are doomed.

---

12. Stott, *Cross of Christ*, 114.

The Beginning of Knowledge

In response to this dilemma, most monotheistic religions perform one of the following maneuvers: In their attempt to set things right with God, they will either claim that *God simply declares that we are forgiven*, or they will offer *salvation by merit of righteous deeds* meant to appease God's wrath. The problem with the former is that debts are never "simply" forgiven. Somebody will always absorb the burden of the debt. Lending your friend your life savings and then forgiving his debt when he is unable to repay it does not miraculously cause the lost money to reappear in your safety deposit box. The old adage that "nothing is ever free in life" is quite true when speaking of matters of salvation. Somebody somewhere must absorb the liability of sin against God. For God to simply ignore the problem of sin would greatly undermine his holiness, mock his sense of justice, and trivialize the gravity of human sin. A holy God who will not tolerate the sulfurous stench of sin does not simply absorb this foul liability, becoming, himself a reeking depository of iniquity. A God who turns a blind eye to crimes against his moral perfection is no God at all. Without proper retribution, God cannot and would not simply declare us righteous, our sins forgiven.

The latter option of salvation by acts of righteousness fares no better than the first because it suggests that a fallen and finite sinner can somehow facilitate his own salvation, which ultimately makes God subject to man's will. This option only removes God from the center of salvation and crowns man as king of his own redemption. But how can a man, steeped in sin and soaked in a depraved nature that affects his entire race, save himself from himself? This would be no different from an attempt to wash the mud from your hands using none other than mud. Imagine such absurdity. The prayers, pilgrimages, and moral restrictions intended to bring man nearer to God do nothing to exonerate sin and achieve only the mockery of God's holiness. Have you seen such men? They clap one another on the back while offering congratulatory words for a job well done. They have earned exactly what their efforts have merited—hell.

Imagine a man whose heart is failing. Rather than go to the hospital to receive the medical expertise of skilled surgeons, this man, who has no medical or anatomical knowledge, decides to perform open heart surgery on himself with large clumsy wooden tools he finds lying about his kitchen. His chances of successfully repairing his heart are so grim, it is inevitable he will die. The idiocy that would incite a man to such a task is the same that would provoke him to repair his own putrid spiritual condition by efforts of works righteousness. Because of sin, humans are in a state of spiritual cardiac arrest, and only the Great Physician, Jesus Christ, can heal their life-threatening predicament.

Imagine the folly of attempting salvation on our own. This is precisely what countless well-intentioned fools have attempted to do throughout the ages. So filled with pride and so offended by the grace of God, these madmen have sought to climb a ladder to heaven. By merit of righteous deeds, they steadily ascend toward heaven, unaware that the ladder of their own "righteous" effort is falling through an abysmal infinity away from God's throne. Have you seen such men? Attempting to pay an infinite debt with mere pennies is not a serious option. Our best efforts are damning at best. That is why there must be another way.

Luke's gospel relates the story of an interaction between Jesus, a Pharisee, and a woman who had lived a life of sin (Luke 7:36–50). The woman, knowing full well the gravity of her sin, approached Jesus in contrition and tears, anointing him with an expensive perfume and worshiping at his feet. But at the site of this dissolute woman, the self-righteous Pharisee was filled with disgust. His thoughts immediately turned to loathing, for no true prophet would let himself be defiled by such a vulgar creature as this woman, whose abhorrent sin was well-known in the community. The irony here is that, being a true prophet, Jesus knew the thoughts of the Pharisee and responded in a parable:

> Two men owed money to a certain moneylender. One owed him five hundred denarii, and the other fifty. Neither of them had money to pay him back, so he canceled the debts of both. (Luke 7:41–42b)

There are several lessons and numerous applications that can be gleaned from this story, but what I would like to highlight here is that both of the debtors in this short parable defaulted on their loans. A denarius was a day's wage, but whether we are speaking of a few coins or a chest of treasure, the point is that neither of the debtors had the means to pay what was owed. Jesus wanted this Pharisee to understand that whether it be a mammoth or a meager debt, one is subject to the mercy of the moneylender. The debt of sin cannot be paid but by the grace of God.

Unlike its monotheistic peers, Christianity neither waives the debt (an offense to God's holiness) nor contemplates the absurdity of letting a penniless man pay his own liability (an offense to God's grace). Rather, it shows how God bore the force of his own wrath and paid in full the debt of sin that man had accumulated against himself (Rom. 5:8–11). The Christian faith asserts that God took the initiative and made possible a restored relationship with him. The coming of Christ—the Word made flesh—reveals that the message of God and subsequent knowledge of him are inseparable from his being.

We fools of this terrestrial loony bin are all seeking restoration in one way or another. We are seeking love, salvation, meaning, and hope. We are all seeking God in different ways, but what counts is not our efforts in seeking him but his efficacy in seeking us. God help us then! For it is God's help alone that can save us.

To believe in Christ as revealed in Scripture is to finally and fully know God. This is the madman's ultimate concern. J.I. Packer puts it this way:

> What were we made for? To know God. What aim should we set ourselves in life? To know God. What is the "eternal life" that Jesus gives? Knowledge of God. What is the best thing in life, bringing more joy, delight and contentment than anything else? Knowledge of God.[13]

But it is not man's initiative that drives him toward knowledge of God. Man's initiative drives him nowhere but deeper into madness. Only when God approaches the madman and loosens the constraints on his mind will he be able to know his Savior and clearly see the reality before him (Eph. 2:4–5). God fills us with knowledge and gives us understanding so we can know him all the more (Phil. 1:9; Col. 1:9; 1 John 5:20). And though God gives us the ability to know him, it is not our knowledge of him but his knowledge of us that saves us (Jer. 24:7; Gal. 4:9). On this point Packer emphasizes the fact that human knowledge of God is secondary to divine knowledge of humans: "All my knowledge of him depends on his sustained initiative in knowing me."[14] To know the Father is to be known by the Father, and to know the Son is to enjoy salvation from the madness of our fallen intellectual state and eternal separation from God. "I know him," says Packer, "because he first knew me, and continues to know me."[15]

Proper knowledge of God begins, thus, with proper knowledge of Jesus, which leads to repentance, which leads to justification (John 7:27–29).[16] Knowledge of the Divine begins with knowledge of the Messiah and

---

13. Packer, *Knowing God*, 33.
14. Ibid., 41.
15. Ibid., 41.
16. Justification in its theological sense refers to our legal standing before God, in

culminates when the believer is ushered into the eternal presence of the triune God (John 4:22–26). But unless Christ seeks us, by the will of the Father, we can never hope to know him (John 10; 2 Tim. 2:19). It is God's Spirit that illuminates to us the reality of our broken, miserable state and empowers us to turn to Christ in belief so that the Father's forgiveness can be savored. To know him, we must not only be known by him, but we must also know the reality of our own fallen condition—a condition from which we must ultimately turn in repentance. Pascal spoke well when he said this:

> Knowing God without knowing our own wretchedness makes for pride.
>
> Knowing our own wretchedness without knowing God makes for despair.
>
> Knowing Jesus Christ strikes the balance because he shows us both God and our own wretchedness.[17]

Spiritual brokenness is much more than an emotional state; it is a reality in which all humans live. We are all spiritually broken. We are in need of spiritual reparation because we do not function correctly. This realization is the first step to repentance and the restoration of the mind (Rom. 12:1–2). Because of God, we can have knowledge. By knowing God, our knowledge can be ever increasingly perfected.

KNOWING RIGHTLY

This brings us to reason's final step: to justifiably believe in the truth of God as specified in his revelation. The convoluted cosmos and hazy hereafter become clear once we see them through eyes enlightened by true knowledge (Eph. 1:18).[18] To affirm knowledge is to affirm God and to stop indulging the stark contradictions and foolish impulses of our insanity. "We cannot know other things rightly without knowing God rightly," says John Frame.[19] When we know God rightly, he becomes for us those indispensable spectacles by which we know the world.

---

which we are declared righteous, or free of guilt. See Fluhrer, *Atonement*.

17. Pascal, *Pensées*, 192/527, 57.

18. See Pearcy, *Total Truth*. Here she makes a good case for the Christian worldview by demonstrating its complete full-orbed explanation of reality.

19. Frame, *Doctrine of Knowledge*, 10.

The Beginning of Knowledge

Look at where we are and from where we have come. We have gasped for air beneath the asphyxiating and fatuous assertions of insanity. We have walked a fine and perilous line, crossing the chasm of skepticism on one side and the abyss of radical rationalism and empiricism on the other. We have resisted the narcotizing and mind-numbing effects of pure fideism and have finally submitted to recognizing our need for an infinite and superbly perfect *Knower*. And to the praise of God's glorious grace, we have come to see that by confessing our belief in the regenerating power of Christ, which works in the hearts and minds of former madmen, knowledge will be restored.

It can be no other way. Christian theism is the solution, not the problem. We have seen, far too often, that when speaking of thoughtful reflection and philosophical rigor, theists are naïvely accused of lacking both. The self-appointed guardians of knowledge—certain religious skeptics, so-called reasonists, and materialists of various philosophical schools—claim to drink deeply from the crystal-clear spring of knowledge. All the while, they accuse their theistic peers of decanting the dregs of idiocy and lapping them up with maddening ferocity. Some laugh and scoff and dance on the grave of the God who was heralded dead long ago by the great prophet of Darwinism, Friedrich Nietzsche, and by his progeny. God is not needed. God is not wanted. And for these searing locutions, the defamers of God are applauded for their cleverness and commitment to reason. But wherever we are bereft of God, we are only left wanting justified true beliefs about reality.

We have seen that Christian theism is neither the antithesis of philosophical reasoning nor the bane of the epistemic project. It is, rather, a clarifying and sanctifying alembic of knowledge that reveals a reality both knowable and worth knowing. The true enemy of reason is the corrupt human heart that engenders enmity toward the all-knowing Knower and Source of knowledge.

Skeptics will surely doubt these truths and contest the facts, but if God is the best explanation for the possibility of knowledge, then his words are surely more trustworthy than those of skeptics like Arthur Schopenhauer who said long ago that "he is still in his childhood who can think that superhuman beings have ever given our race information about the aim of its existence or that of the world."[20] Ironically, Schopenhauer may have been more right than he guessed, for we should all believe our God with the

---

20. Schopenhauer, *Horrors and Absurdities*, 66.

faith of a little child and know our God with the mind of a grown man (1 Cor. 14:20). An adult must reason and weigh the evidence before him. He must falter, reaffirm, and then doubt again as he reassesses and synthesizes the world of ideas, all the while building a tower of knowledge. But only when the childlike hand of faith grasps his own and leads him forward will man show the world his confidence in the knowledge he has. If we cannot trust God like a child, whatever knowledge of God we have will only prove inadequate for our salvation.

The necessity of God's special revelation in Scripture and in the Christ to which it points renders fruitless the claims of any other would-be revelation. This is not to say that Christ-less people will have no chance at *knowing*. What it tells us is that of the various achievable levels of knowledge, the most profound and satisfying of all can only be enjoyed by those who know Jesus Christ. Justified true beliefs of this kind are implanted in us and revealed in the Word made text, which unveils the saving knowledge of Jesus Christ, the Word made flesh. Beneath this highest sphere of knowledge is a second category of knowledge: that made clear by the *common grace* of God that works among *all* men and allows them to accomplish significant understanding about both God and the universe in which they live. Finally, beneath this general knowledge of the world, we find a third sphere containing the lies and falsehood, deception and intellectual corruption that affect the minds of the unregenerate while vying to control the minds of those redeemed by Christ.

All of us will spend a majority of our intellectual life somewhere in the second sphere, enjoying knowledge about the world acquired by our common sense efforts of observation and rational reflection. Only those who know Christ, however, will venture into the first sphere while working to be rid of the third with its misplaced perceptions of the world. Those who do not know Christ will shirk the first—even despise it—while frequenting the madhouse of the third. In essence, those who do not know Christ do not have complete knowledge of ultimate reality and cannot be expected to think like those who do. They are bound to certain spiritual, moral, emotional, and intellectual uncertainties that do not touch the redeemed.

This truth can both soothe and irritate, but it should by no means undermine the reality that the Christian worldview is the only belief system by which we will ever understand *why* we know what we know. Sure, we can possess knowledge without knowing God, but without knowing God we can never truly know *how* we possess any knowledge. Let us know him then and enjoy the riches of his knowledge. As a psalmist puts it: "The fear of the Lord is the beginning of wisdom" (Ps. 111:10).

Have you seen such men—regenerated by the Spirit, saved by the cross of the Son, and brought into relationship with the eternal Father by the grace of God through faith in Jesus Christ? Have you seen these former madmen, now enlightened to knowledge of the triune God as they rejoice with hearts full of thanksgiving and praise? Freed from the lamentable lunacy that once limited their grasp of reality, they can only laugh at the antics of their former way of life, before knowledge, before God. They are now known by God, and as they come to know him more, the layers of insanity are meticulously incised, revealing the world with ever-increasing clarity. Have you seen such men, released from the confines of insanity?

Bibliography

Ayer, A.J. "The Verification Method and Elimination of Metaphysics." In *The Theory of Knowledge: Classic and Contemporary Readings*, edited by Louis P. Pojman, 468–75. 3rd ed. Belmont, CA: Wadsworth, 2003.
Benatar, David. *Better Never to Have Been: The Harm of Coming into Existence*. New York: Oxford University Press, 2006.
Berkeley, George. *A Treatise Concerning the Principles of Human Knowledge*.
Blamires, Harry. *The Post-Christian Mind*. Vancouver: Regent College Publishing, 2003.
Blomberg, Craig. *The Historical Reliability of the Gospels*. 2nd ed. Downers Grove, IL: InterVarsity, 2007.
Bruce, F.F. *The Canon of Scripture*. Downers Grove, IL: InterVarsity, 1988.
Carson, D.A and John D. Woodbridge. *Hermeneutics, Authority, and Canon*. Eugene, OR: Wipf and Stock, 2005.
Calvin, John. *Institutes of the Christian Religion*. Translated by Henry Beveridge. 1845. Peabody, MA: Hendrickson Publishers, 2008.
Chesterton, G.K. *Orthodoxy*. New York: Image, 2001.
Chisholm, Roderick. "The Problem of the Criterion." In *The Theory of Knowledge: Classical and Contemporary Readings*, edited by Louis P. Pojman, 9–18. 3rd ed. Belmont, CA: Wadsworth, 2003.
Clark, Gordon. *Thales to Dewey: A History of Philosophy*. 4th ed. The Trinity Foundation, 2000.
Clifford, William K. *The Ethics of Belief and other Essays*. Amherst, NY: Prometheus Books, 1999.
Comte-Sponville, André. *L'Esprit de l'athéisme: Introduction à une spiritualité sans Dieu*. Paris: Albin Michel, 2006.
Copleston, Frederick. *Greece and Rome: A History of Philosophy*, vol. 1. London: Search Press, 1946.
———. *Descartes to Leibniz: A History of Philosophy*, vol. 4. London: Search Press, 1958.
Craig, William Lane and J.P. Moreland. *Philosophical Foundations for a Christian Worldview*. Downers Grove, IL: InterVarsity, 2003.
Dawkins, Richard. *A Devil's Chaplain: Reflections on Hope, Lies, Science, and Love*. Boston: Houghton Mifflin, 2003.
———. "Science verses Religion." In *Philosophy of Religion: An Anthology*, edited by Louis J. Pojman, 451–54. 4th ed. Belmont, CA: Wadsworth, 2003.

Bibliography

Demarest, Bruce A. and Gordon R. Lewis. *Integrative Theology.* Vol. 1. Grand Rapids, MI: Zondervan, 1996.

Dennett, Daniel C. *Breaking the Spell: Religion as a Natural Phenomenon.* New York: Penguin, 2006.

Descartes, René. *Discourse on Method and Meditations on First Philosophy.* Translated by Donald A. Cress, 4th ed. Indianapolis: Hackett, 1998.

DeWeese, Garret. "Theology and Science: Converge on Reality." *Christian Research Journal* 35, no. 1 (2012): 36–39.

———. *Doing Philosophy as a Christian.* Downers Grove IL: InterVarsity, 2011.

Diegenes Laertius, *Lives of Eminent Philosophers.*

Edwards, Jonathan. *The Images of Divine Things.* Edited by Perry Miller. New Haven, CT: Yale University Press, 1948.

Ereira, Alan and Terry Jones. *Terry Jones' Medieval Lives.* London: BBC Books, 2004.

Evans, C. Stephen. *Faith Beyond Reason: A Kierkegaardian Account.* Grand Rapids, MI: William B. Eerdmans, 1998.

Ferry, Luc. *A Brief History of Thought: A Philosophical Guide to Living.* Translated by Theo Cuffe. 2010. New York: Harper Perennial, 2011.

Ferry, Luc and Lucien Jerphagnon. *La tentation du christianisme.* Paris: Bernard Grasset, 2009.

Fluhrer, Gabriel N. E., ed. *Atonement.* Phillipsburg, N.J.: P & R, 2010.

Fogelin, Robert. *Walking the Tightrope of Reason: The Precarious Life of a Rational Animal.* New York, Oxford University Press, 2003.

Frame, John M. *The Doctrine of the Knowledge of God.* Phillipsburg, NJ: P & R, 1987.

———. *The Doctrine of the Word of God.* Phillipsburg, NJ: P & R, 2010.

Frankfurt, Harry G. *On Bullshit.* Princeton, NJ: Princeton University Press, 2005.

Gettier, Edmund L. "Is Justified True Belief Knowledge?" In *The Theory of Knowledge: Classic and Contemporary Readings,* edited by Louis P. Pojman, 125-26. 3rd ed. Belmont, CA: Wadsworth, 2003.

Goldman, Emma. "The Philosophy of Atheism." In *The Portable Atheist, Essential Readings for the Nonbeliever,* edited by Christopher Hitchens, 129-33. Philadelphia: Da Capo, 2007.

Groothuis, Douglas. *Christian Apologetics: A Comprehensive Case for Christian Faith.* Downers Grove, IL: InterVarsity, 2011.

———. *Truth Decay: Defending Christianity Against the Challenge of Postmodernism,* Downers Grove, IL: InterVaristy, 2000.

———. "Questioning Hume's Theory of Meaning," in *Kinesis*, 18:2 (1992).

Grudem, Wayne. *Systematic Theology: An Introduction to Biblical Doctrine.* Grand Rapids, MI: Zondervan, 1994.

Gula, Robert J. *Nonsense: Red Herrings, Straw Men, and Sacred Cows: How We Abuse Logic in Our Everyday Language.* Mount Jackson, VA: Axios, 2007.

Haddad, Jonah. *Leaving Dirt Place: Love as an Apologetic for Christianity.* Eugene, OR: Wipf and Stock, 2011.

Hawking, Stephen and Leonard Mlodinow. *The Grand Design.* New York: Bantam, 2010.

Heidegger, Martin. *Being and Time.*

Helm, Paul. *Faith and Understanding.* Grand Rapids, MI: William B. Eerdmans, 1997.

Holmes, Arthur. *Fact, Value, and God.* Grand Rapids, MI.: William B. Eerdmans, 1997.

Hume, David. *An Enquiry Concerning Human Understanding.* Mineola, NY: Dover, 2004.

———. *Dialogues Concerning Natural Religion.*

Bibliography

James, William. "The Will to Believe." In *Classics of Philosophy*, edited by Louis P. Pojman, 1077–84. 2nd ed. New York: Oxford University Press, 2003.

Jones, W.T. *A History of Western Philosophy: The Classical Mind*, 2nd ed. New York: Harcourt Brace Jovanovich College Publishers, 1970.

Julius Caesar, *The Gallic Wars*, translated by W. A. McDevitte and W. S. Bohn. 1869. New York: Harper and Brothers, 1869.

Kierkegaard, Søren. *Provocations: The Spiritual Writings of Kierkegaard*, edited and compiled by Charles E. Moore. Maryknoll, NY: Orbis Books, 2003.

———. "Subjectivity is Truth." In *Philosophy of Religion: An Anthology*, edited by Louis J. Pojman, 378–86. 4th ed. Belmont, CA: Wadsworth, 2003.

Leibniz, Gottfried Wilhelm. *Monadology*.

Lennox, John. *God and Stephen Hawking: Whose Design is it Anyway?* Oxford: Lion Hudson, 2011.

Locke, John. *An Essay Concerning Human Understanding*, edited by Roger Woolhouse. Revised ed. London: Penguin Books, 2004.

Malcolm, Norman. "The Groundlessness of Belief." In *Philosophy of Religion: An Anthology*, edited by Louis J. Pojman, 391–98. 4th ed. Belmont, CA: Wadsworth, 2003.

McGrath, Alister. *A Fine Tuned Universe: The Quest for God in Science and Theology*. Louisville, KY: Westminster John Knox, 2011.

———. *Mere Apologetics: How to Help Seekers and Skeptics Find Faith*. Grand Rapids, MI: Baker, 2011.

McGrew, Timothy. *The Foundations of Knowledge*. Lanham, MD: Littlefield Adams, 1995.

———. "A Defense of Classical Foundationalism." In *The Theory of Knowledge: Classical and Contemporary Readings*, edited by Louis P. Pojman, 194–205. 3rd ed. Belmont, CA: Wadsworth, 2003.

Metzger, Bruce M. *The Canon of the New Testament: Its Origin, Development, and Significance*. Oxford: Oxford University Press, 1987.

Moore, G.E. "A Defense of Common Sense." In *The Theory of Knowledge: Classical and Contemporary Readings*, edited by Louis P. Pojman, 49–55. 3rd ed. Belmont, CA: Wadsworth, 2003.

Moreland, J.P. *Love Your God With All Your Mind: The Role of Reason in the Life of the Soul*. 2nd ed. Colorado Springs, CO: NavPress, 2012.

———. "Truth, Contemporary Philosophy, and the Postmodern Turn." *Journal of the Evangelical Theological Society*, 48:1 (March 2005): 77–88.

Meyer, Stephen C. *Signature in the Cell: DNA and the Evidence for Intelligent Design*. New York: Harper One, 2009.

Nichols, Stephen J. *The Reformation: How a Monk and a Mallet Changed the World*. Wheaton, IL: Crossway, 2007.

Packer, J.I. *Knowing God*. 20th anniversary ed. Downers Grove, IL: InterVarsity, 1993.

Paley, William. *Natural Theology*. Oxford, England: Oxford University Press, 2006.

Pascal, Blaise. *Pensées*. Translated by A.J. Krailsheimer. 2nd ed. 1966. London: Penguin, 1995.

Peirce, Charles Sanders. *Collected Papers*. Edited by Charles Harthorne and Paul Weiss, 8 vols. Cambridge, MA: Harvard University Press, 1960.

Penelhum, Terence. *God and Skepticism*. Boston: D. Reidel, 1983.

Pearcy, Nancy. *Total Truth*. Study guide ed. Wheaton, IL: Crossway, 2005.

Plantinga, Alvin. *Warranted Christian Belief*. New York: Oxford University Press, 2000.

———. *Warrant and Proper Function*. New York: Oxford University Press, 1993.

Bibliography

Plantinga Alvin, and Michael Tooley. *Knowledge of God*. Malden, MA: Blackwell, 2008.

Plato, *The Apology*.

Pojman, Louis. *What can we Know: An Introduction to the Theory of Knowledge*. 2nd ed. Belmont, CA: Wadsworth, 2001.

Popkin, Richard H. *The History of Scepticism from Erasmus to Spinoza*. Berkeley, CA: University of California Press, 1979.

Reid, Thomas. *Inquiry into the Human Mind on the Principles of Common Sense*.

Rosenberg, Alex. *The Atheist's Guide to Reality: Enjoying Life without Illusions*. New York: W.W. Norton and Company, 2011.

Russell, Bertrand. "An Outline of Intellectual Rubbish." In *The Portable Atheist: Essential Readings for the Nonbeliever*, edited by Christopher Hitchens, 181–206. Philadelphia: Da Capo, 2007.

———. "A Free Man's Worship." In *Moral Philosophy: A Reader*, edited by Louis P. Pojman, 313–17. 3rd ed. Indianapolis, IN: Hackett, 2003.

Schmidt, Alvin J. *How Christianity Changed the World*. Grand Rapids, MI: Zondervan, 2004.

Schopenhauer, Arthur. *The Horrors and Absurdities of Religion*. Translated by R.J. Hollingdale 1970. London: Penguin Books, 2009.

Scull, Andrew. *Madness: A Very Short Introduction*. Oxford: Oxford University Press: 2011.

Sennett, James F. "Hume's Stopper and the Natural Theology Project." In *In Defense of Natural Theology: A Post-Humean Assessment*, edited by Douglas Groothuis and James F. Sennett. Downers Grove, IL: InterVarsity Press, 2005.

Sextus Empiricus. *Outlines in Skepticism*. Translated by Julia Annas and Jonathan Barnes. Cambridge: Cambridge University Press, 2000.

Smith, R. Scott. *Naturalism and our Knowledge of Reality: Testing Religious Truth-claims*. Burlington, VT: Ashgate, 2012.

Spinoza, Baruch. "Ethic." In *Classics of Philosophy*, edited by Louis P. Pojman, 571–617. 2nd ed. New York: Oxford University Press, 2003.

Sproul, R.C. *Chosen by God*. Wheaton, IL: Tyndale House, 1986.

———. *The Holiness of God*. 2nd ed. Weaton, IL: Tyndale House, 1998.

Stark, Rodney. *The Victory of Reason: How Christianity Led to Freedom, Capitalism, and Western Success*. New York: Random House, 2005.

Stott, John. *The Authority of the Bible*. Downers Grove, IL; InterVarsity, 1974.

———. *The Cross of Christ*, 20th anniversary ed. Downers Grove, IL: InterVarsity, 2006.

———. *Your Mind Matters*. Downers Grove, IL: InterVarsity, 2006.

Striker, Gisela. "Historical Reflections on Claissical Pyrrhonism and Neo-Pyrrhonism." In *Pyrrhonian Skepticism*, edited by Walter Sinnott-Armstrong, 13–24. New York: Oxford University Press, 2004.

Stroud, Barry. "Contemporary Pyrrhonism." In *Pyrrhonian Skepticism*, edited by Walter Sinnott-Armstrong, 174–87. New York: Oxford University Press, 2004.

Suzuki, D.T. *What is Zen?* New York; Harper & Row, 1971.

Swinburne, Richard. "Teleological Arguments." In *The Existence of God*. 2nd ed. Oxford: Oxford University Press, 2004.

Tallis, Raymond. "What Neuroscience Cannot Tell Us About Ourselves." *The New Atlantis*, 29, Fall (2010): 3–25.

Van Voorst, Robert E, ed. "Dhammacakkapparattana Sutta." In *Anthology of World Scriptures*. 5th ed. Belmont, CA: Wadsworth, 2006.

Bibliography

Wells, Peter S. *Barbarians to Angels: The Dark Ages Reconsidered.* New York: W.W. Norton and Company, 2008.

White, Steven A. "Pyrrho of Elis." In *Cambridge Dictionary of Philosophy*, edited by Robert Audi, 760. 2nd ed. Cambridge: Cambridge University Press, 1999.

General Index

aboutness, 74, 138
Abraham, 93-94
Academy, 21
Adam and Eve, 23-24, 53, 107, 129-30
Agrippa, 22
Alexander the Great, 16
a priori, 40, 51, 61
Arcesilaus, 21-22
Aristotle, 12, 35, 108
ataraxia, 17-18, 20-23, 27, 30, 39
Athens, 100
Ayer, A.J., 67

basic belief, 49, 60
Berkeley, George, 25, 52, 111
best explanation, 89, 105, 121-22, 145
Blamires, Harry, 88-89
blind leap, 88, 90-93
Book of Nature, 123
Buddhism, 22-23, 28

Calvin, John, 35, 125-26, 133, 136
Chesterton, G.K., 62-63, 76
Chisholm, Roderick, 37, 103-5
Cicero, 31
Clark, Gordon, 43, 50
Clifford, William K., 93
cogito ergo sum, 43, 49, 102
common grace, 78, 146
common sense, 26, 58-62, 67, 108, 113, 146
common sense realism, 59, 108, 135
contingency, 109, 118
Copernicus, Nicolaus, 107
Copleston, Frederick, 22, 40-41, 50-51

correspondence view of truth, 5, 9, 59, 134
cosmological argument, 118-20
Craig, William Lane, 69-70, 118

dark age, 55
Dawkins, Richard, 76-77, 89, 107
deductive arguments, 117-18, 120-22
deism, 110
Dennett, Daniel C., 66-67
Descartes, René, 25, 40-44, 49-54, 72, 77, 90, 101-4
design inference, 122-23
design plan, 9
Diet of Worms, 34
Diogenes Laertius, 21, 31
Dickens, Charles, 19
dogmatism, 21, 31, 34, 55, 57, 66, 103-5, 116, 137

Ecclesiast, 23
Edwards, Jonathan, 104, 124
Enlightenment, 7, 30-31, 47-60, 72, 77, 81, 88-89, 102, 120
Epicurean, 19
episteme, 8
epistemology, ix, 8, 11, 14, 18, 25, 30, 38-39, 44, 51, 56-61, 80
Erasmus of Rotterdam, 35
ethics, ix, 44, 112
Evans, C. Stephen, 87-88

faithism, 87-88
Fantin-Latour, Henri, 8-9
Ferry, Luc, 89

General Index

fideism, 14, 81, 87–91, 96–98
flying spaghetti monster, 80, 98
foundationalism, 60
four noble truths, 23
Frame, John M., 126, 129, 144
Frankfurt, Harry, 7, 45

Gettier, Edmund L., 8
God
   Creator, 25, 53, 91, 101, 106, 110, 112–15, 120, 123–31, 135, 139
   Designer, 115, 122–23
   Divine Mind, 117
   Knower, ix, 14, 101, 110, 145
   Knowledge-giver, 126
   Source of knowledge, ix, 25, 78, 91, 102–3, 106–9, 112–13, 135, 145
   triune, 138, 144, 147
god of the gaps, 102
Goldman, Emma, 66
Groothuis, Douglas, ix, 13, 57, 102, 123
Grudem, Wayne, 128–30, 136
Gula, Robert J., 62

Hawking, Stephen, 107, 116
Helm, Paul, 90–93
Hume, David, 25–29, 52, 56–59, 61, 67, 104

inductive arguments, 123
intentionality, 74–76

James, William, 13, 46
Jesus
   Logos, 139
   Messiah, 94, 137, 143
   Savoir, ix, 137, 143
   Word made flesh, 133–34, 137–39, 143, 146
Job, 124–25
John, apostle, 94
Jones, W.T., 21
Julius Caesar, 108
justified true belief, 8, 17, 36, 53, 58, 70, 74, 76–77, 81, 86, 91, 95, 98, 101–7, 112–15, 120–23, 127, 133–34, 145–46

Kant, Immanuel, 57–59, 61
Kepler, Johannes, 107
Kierkegaard, Søren, 88–92, 101
know thyself, 38–39
Knox, John, 35

La Lecture, 8–9
Leibniz, Gottfried Wilhelm, 25, 51–52, 74, 118
Lennox, John, 77, 116
Locke, John, 11, 25, 52, 120
logical necessity, 9, 76, 103, 118–19, 135
logos, 8, 139
lumière naturelle, 49
Luther, Martin, 32–36, 40–43, 101

Malcolm, Norman, 90
materialism,
   methodological, 116
   philosophical, 55, 65–68, 72–75, 79, 102
Matthew, apostle, 94
McGrath, Alister, 121–22
mental states, 74–75
metaphysics, ix, 25–26, 49, 58–60, 68
Montaigne, Michel de, 36–37, 40–41
Moore, G.E., 60
moral argument, 118
moral knowledge, 24, 28–29, 129
moral law, 6, 128
Moreland, J.P., 38, 59, 69–70, 95

naked teachers, 16–18, 22
natural revelation, 122
natural theology, 115–18, 120–24, 126–31
New Testament, 135, 137
Newton, Isaac, 107
Ninety-five Theses, 33
nondualism, pantheistic, 22

Old Testament, 94, 137
ontological argument, 118

Packer, J.I., 143
Paley, William, 115–17, 123
Pandora's Box, 36
pantheism, 51

General Index

Pascal, Blaise, 10, 52, 104, 107, 112, 125, 136, 144
Pasteur, Louis, 117
Paul, apostle, 61, 76, 85, 110, 125, 136
philosophy, ix, 16–17, 22–23, 26–28, 38–44, 48, 56–59, 65, 77, 89–90, 102, 106–7, 112, 118, 139
Plantinga, Alvin, 9, 68–74
Plato, 8, 21, 101
Popkin, Richard H., 33
principle of sufficient reason, 118
problem of the criterion, 34, 37–38
proper function, 68–72, 75, 106, 123
Pyrrho of Elis, 16–18, 22–23, 25, 29, 40, 71–72, 101
Pyrrhonian, 17–19, 21–29, 36, 45–46, 135
Pyrrhonism, 22–23, 27, 29, 32–33, 41

radical empiricism, 66–67, 73–77, 86, 97, 102, 104–6, 113, 120
reasonism, 86
reasonist, 73, 76, 145
Reformation, 30–34, 36, 41
Reid, Thomas, 26, 59–60
Rosenberg, Alex, 74
Russell, Bertrand, 10, 65–67

Satan, 24, 53, 130
Schopenhauer, Arthur, 89, 107, 145
scientism, 55, 66, 107
Sennett, James F., 119
sensus divinitatis, 125–26
Sextus Empiricus, 17–18, 31, 40

Skepticism, 6, 9, 13–14, 16–19, 21–30, 32–46, 51–54, 58–61, 67, 71–72, 75, 85–86, 97, 101–4, 11, 113, 116, 123, 145
Socrates, 21–22, 39
Sophists, 16, 19, 86
special revelation, 81, 134–35, 137–38, 146
Spinoza, Baruch, 51–52
Spoul, R.C., 97, 139
Stoicism, 21–22
Stott, John, 95, 135, 140
Striker, Gisela, 17

Tallis, Raymond, 73
Timon, 18
theory of knowledge, ix, 8, 11–13, 16, 27, 29, 111
Thomas, apostle, 94, 101
Thomas Aquinas, 36, 118
transcendental idealism, 58
tripartite analysis, 8–10, 17, 58, 91

warrant, 9–10, 18, 69, 103
Westminster Confession of Faith, 110, 130
Word
 made flesh, 133–34, 137–39, 143, 146
 made text, 134, 137, 146
 of God, 34–35, 136–37

Zen, 112
Zwingli, Ulrich, 35

Scripture Index

GENESIS

1:27–31	96
1:27	124
3	24, 53, 129
3:1	24
3:3	24
3:5	53
3:15	53

EXODUS

33:12–13	136

LEVITICUS

1:44–45	139
19:2	139

DEUTERONOMY

4:2	137
8:3	136

2 SAMUEL

22:31	136

JOB

9:8–10	124–25
38	125

PSALMS

8	96
8:4–8	129
19:1–2	124
111:10	146
119:66–67	136
119:105	136

PROVERBS

2:1–8	110
8:1–3	111
8:4	111
8:6–7	111
8:23	111
15:14	111
18:15	111
20:15	111
30:5–6	137

ECCLESIASTES

1:17–18	123

Scripture Index

ISAIAH

59:2	140
64:6	140

JEREMIAH

24:7	143

LUKE

7:36–50	142
7:41–42b	142
24:44	135

JOHN

1:1	138–39
1:14	133, 138–39
4:22–26	144
5:39	135
7:27–29	143
8:34	130
10	144
14:6	139
16:12–13	135
17:3	139
18:37–38	139
20	94
20:29	94

ROMANS

1:20–21	125
1:25	129
1:28	129
3:9–18	140
3:10–18	129
5:8–11	143
5:12–21	129
10:13–17	137
11:36	110
12:1–2	22, 144
12:2	112

1 CORINTHIANS

1:18–31	76
1:20	61
1:21	62
14:20	146

2 CORINTHIANS

4:2	136

GALATIANS

1–2	135
4:9	143

EPHESIANS

1:17–18	136
1:17–21	110
1:18	144
2:1–2	95
2:4–5	143
4:13	136
4:17–19	6, 29

PHILIPPIANS

1:9	143
2:5–11	139
3:7–8	35

COLOSSIANS

1:9	143
2:2–3	139

2 TIMOTHY

2:19	144

HEBREWS

1:1	133
4:12	134
11:1	93

1 PETER

1:16	139

2 PETER

1:20–21	135

1 JOHN

5:20	143

REVELATION

4:11	110
20:2	53
22:18–19	137

www.ingramcontent.com/pod-product-compliance
Lightning Source LLC
Chambersburg PA
CBHW051937160426
43198CB00013B/2192